117

D1079375

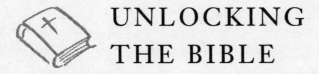

UNLOCKING THE BIBLE

OLD TESTAMENT BOOK IV

Decline and Fall of an Empire

UNLOCKING THE BIBLE

OLD TESTAMENT BOOK IV

Decline and Fall of an Empire

David Pawson

with Andy Peck

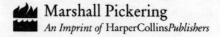

Marshall Pickering
An Imprint of HarperCollins*Publishers*

Marshall Pickering is an Imprint of
HarperCollins*Religious*
Part of HarperCollins*Publishers*
77–85 Fulham Palace Road, London W6 8JB
www.christian-publishing.com

First published in Great Britain in 2000
by Marshall Pickering

1 3 5 7 9 10 8 6 4 2

Copyright © 2000 David Pawson

David Pawson asserts the moral right to be
identified as the author of this work

A catalogue record for this book is
available from the British Library

ISBN 0 551 03191 3

Printed and bound in Great Britain by
Omnia Books Limited, Glasgow

CONDITIONS OF SALE
This book is sold subject to the condition that it
shall not, by way of trade or otherwise, be lent, re-sold,
hired out or otherwise circulated without the publisher's
prior consent in any form of binding or cover other
than that in which it is published and without a
similar condition including this condition
being imposed on the subsequent purchaser.

All rights reserved. No part of this publication may be
reproduced, stored in a retrieval system, or transmitted,
in any form or by any means, electronic, mechanical,
photocopying, recording or otherwise, without the prior
permission of the publishers.

CONTENTS

INTRODUCTION

I suppose this all started in Arabia, in 1957. I was then a chaplain in the Royal Air Force, looking after the spiritual welfare of all those who were not C.E. (Church of England) or R.C. (Roman Catholic) but O.D. (other denominations – Methodist to Salvationist, Buddhist to atheist). I was responsible for a string of stations from the Red Sea to the Persian Gulf. In most there was not even a congregation to call a 'church', never mind a building.

In civilian life I had been a Methodist minister working anywhere from the Shetland Islands to the Thames Valley. In that denomination it was only necessary to prepare a few sermons each quarter, which were hawked around a 'circuit' of chapels. Mine had mostly been of the 'text' type (talking about a single verse) or the 'topic' type (talking about a single subject with many verses from all over the Bible). In both I was as guilty as any of taking texts out of context before I realized that chapter and verse numbers were neither inspired nor intended by God and had done immense damage to Scripture, not least by changing the meaning of 'text' from a whole book to a single sentence. The Bible had become a compendium of 'proof-texts', picked out at will and used to support almost anything a preacher wanted to say.

With a pocketful of sermons based on this questionable technique, I found myself in uniform, facing very different congregations – all male instead of the lifeboat-style gatherings I had been used to: women and children first. My meagre stock of messages soon ran out. Some of them had gone down like a lead balloon, especially in compulsory parade services in England before I was posted overseas.

So here I was in Aden, virtually starting a church from scratch, from the Permanent Staff and temporary National Servicemen of Her Majesty's youngest armed service. How could I get these men interested in the Christian faith and then committed to it?

Something (I would now say: Someone) prompted me to announce that I would give a series of talks over a few months, which would take us right through the Bible ('from Generation to Revolution'!).

It was to prove a voyage of discovery for all of us. The Bible became a new book when seen as a whole. To use a well-worn cliché, we had failed to see the wood for the trees. Now God's plan and purpose were unfolding in a fresh way. The men were getting something big enough to sink their teeth into. The thought of being part of a cosmic rescue was a powerful motivation. The Bible story was seen as both real and relevant.

Of course, my 'overview' was at that time quite simple, even naive. I felt like that American tourist who 'did' the British Museum in 20 minutes – and could have done it in 10 if he'd had his running shoes! We raced through the centuries, giving some books of the Bible little more than a passing glance.

But the results surpassed my expectations and set the course for the rest of my life and ministry. I had become a 'Bible teacher', albeit in embryo. My ambition to share the excitement of knowing the whole Bible became a passion.

When I returned to 'normal' church life, I resolved to take my congregation through the whole Bible in a decade (if they put up with me that long). This involved tackling about one 'chapter' at every service. This took a lot of time, both in preparation (an hour in the study for every 10 minutes in the pulpit) and delivery (45–50 minutes). The ratio was similar to that of cooking and eating a meal.

The effect of this systematic 'exposition' of Scripture confirmed its rightness. A real hunger for God's Word was revealed. People began to *come* from far and wide, 'to recharge their batteries' as some explained. Soon this traffic was reversed. Tape recordings, first prepared for the sick and housebound, now began to *go* far and wide, ultimately in hundreds of thousands to 120 countries. No one was more surprised than I.

Leaving Gold Hill in Buckinghamshire for Guildford in Surrey, I found myself sharing in the design and building of the Millmead Centre, which contained an ideal auditorium for continuing this teaching ministry. When it was opened, we decided to associate it with the whole Bible by reading it aloud right through without stopping. It took us 84 hours, from Sunday evening until Thursday morning, each person reading for 15 minutes before passing the Bible on to someone else. We used the 'Living' version, the easiest both to read and to listen to, with the heart as well as the mind.

We did not know what to expect, but the event seemed to capture the public imagination. Even the mayor wanted to take part and by sheer coincidence (or providence) found himself reading about a husband who was 'well known, for he sits in the council chamber with the other civic leaders' (Proverbs 31:23). He insisted on taking a copy home for his wife. Another lady dropped in on her way to see her solicitor about the legal termination of her marriage and found herself reading, 'I hate divorce, says the Lord'. She never went to the lawyer.

An aggregate of 2,000 people attended and bought half a ton of Bibles. Some came for half an hour and were still there hours later, muttering to themselves, 'Well, maybe just one more book and then I really must go.'

It was the first time many, including our most regular attenders, had ever heard a book of the Bible read straight through. In most churches only a few sentences are read each week and then not always consecutively. What other book would get anyone interested, much less excited, if treated in this way?

So on Sundays we worked through the whole Bible book by book. For the Bible is not one book, but many – in fact, it is a whole library (the word *biblia* in Latin and Greek is plural: 'books'). And not just many books, but many *kinds* of books – history, law, letters, songs, etc. It became necessary, when we had finished studying one book, and were starting on another, to begin with a special introduction covering very basic questions: What kind of book is this? When was it written? Who wrote it? Who was it written for? Above all, *why* was it written? The answer to that last question provided the 'key' to unlock its message. Nothing in that book could be fully understood unless seen as part of the whole. The context of every 'text' was not just the paragraph or the section but fundamentally the whole book itself.

By now, I was becoming more widely known as a Bible teacher and was invited to colleges, conferences and conventions – at first in this country, but increasingly overseas, where tapes had opened doors and prepared the way. I enjoy meeting new people and seeing new places, but the novelty of sitting in a jumbo jet wears off in 10 minutes!

Everywhere I went I found the same eager desire to know God's Word. I praised God for the invention of recording cassettes which, unlike video systems, are standardized the world over. They were helping to plug a real hole in so many places. There is so much successful evangelism but so little teaching ministry to stabilize, develop and mature converts.

I might have continued along these lines until the end of my active ministry, but the Lord had another surprise for me, which was the last link in the chain that led to the publication of these volumes.

In the early 1990s, Bernard Thompson, a friend pastoring a church in Wallingford, near Oxford, asked me to speak at a short series of united meetings with the aim of increasing interest in and knowledge of the Bible – an objective guaranteed to hook me!

I said I would come once a month and speak for three hours about one book in the Bible (with a coffee break in the middle!). In return, I asked those attending to read that book right through before and after my visit. During the following weeks preachers were to base their sermons and house group discussions on the same book. All this would hopefully mean familiarity at least with that one book.

My purpose was two-fold. On the one hand, to get people so interested in that book that they could hardly wait to read it. On the other hand, to give them enough insight and information so that when they did read it they would be excited by their ability to understand it. To help with both, I used pictures, charts, maps and models.

This approach really caught on. After just four months I was pressed to book dates for the next five years, to cover all 66 books! I laughingly declined, saying I might be in heaven long before then (in fact, I have rarely booked anything more than six months ahead, not wanting to mortgage the future, or presume that I have one). But the Lord had other plans and enabled me to complete the marathon.

Anchor Recordings (72, The Street, Kennington, Ashford, Kent TN24 9HS) have distributed my tapes for the last 20 years and when the Director, Jim Harris, heard the recordings of these meetings, he urged me to consider putting them on video. He arranged for cameras and crew to come to High Leigh Conference Centre, its main hall 'converted' into a studio, for three days at a time, enabling 18 programmes to be made with an invited audience. It took another five years to complete this project, which was distributed under the title 'Unlocking the Bible'.

Now these videos are travelling around the world. They are being used in house groups, churches, colleges, the armed forces, gypsy camps, prisons and on cable television networks. During an extended visit to Malaysia, they were being snapped up at a rate of a thousand a week. They have infiltrated all six continents, including Antarctica!

More than one have called this my 'legacy to the church'. Certainly it is the fruit of many years' work. And I am now in my seventieth year on planet earth, though I do not think the Lord has finished with me yet. But I did think this particular task had reached its conclusion. I was mistaken.

HarperCollins approached me with a view to publishing this material in a series of volumes. For the last decade or so I had been writing books for other publishers, so was already convinced that this was a good means of spreading God's Word. Nevertheless, I had two huge reservations about this proposal which made me very hesitant. One was due to the way the material had been prepared and the other related to the way it had been delivered. I shall explain them in reverse order.

First, I have never written out in full any sermon, lecture or talk. I speak from notes, sometimes pages of them. I have been concerned about communication as much as content and intuitively knew that a full manuscript interrupts the rapport between speaker and audience, not least by diverting his eyes from the listeners. Speech that is more spontaneous can respond to reactions as well as express more emotions.

The result is that my speaking and writing styles are very different, each adapted to its own function. I enjoy listening to my tapes and can be deeply moved by myself. I am enthusiastic about reading one of my new publications, often telling my wife, 'This really *is* good stuff!' But when I read a transcript of what I have said, I am ashamed and even appalled. Such repetition of words and phrases! Such rambling, even incomplete sentences! Such a mixture of verb tenses, particularly past and present! Do I really abuse the Queen's English like this? The evidence is irrefutable.

I made it clear that I could not possibly contemplate writing out all this material in full. It has taken most of one lifetime anyway and I do not have another. True, transcripts of the talks had already been made, with a view to translating and dubbing the videos into other languages such as Spanish and Chinese. But the thought of these being printed as they were horrified me. Perhaps this is a final struggle with pride, but the contrast with my written books, over which I took such time and trouble, was more than I could bear.

I was assured that copy editors correct most grammatical blunders. But the main remedy proposed was to employ a 'ghostwriter' who was in tune with me and my ministry, to adapt the material for printing. An introduction to the person chosen, Andy Peck, gave me every confidence that he could do the job, even though the result would not be what I would have written – nor, for that matter, what he would have written himself.

I gave him all the notes, tapes, videos and transcripts, but these volumes are as much his work as mine. He has worked incredibly hard and I am deeply grateful to him for enabling me to reach many more with the truth that sets people free. If one gets a prophet's reward for merely giving the prophet a drink of water, I can only thank the Lord for the reward Andy will get for this immense labour of love.

Second, I have never kept careful records of my sources. This is partly because the Lord blessed me with a reasonably good memory for such things as quotations and illustrations and perhaps also because I have never used secretarial assistance.

Books have played a major role in my work – three tons of them, according to the last furniture remover we employed, filling two rooms and a garden shed. They are in three categories: those I have read, those I intend to read and those I will never read! They have been such a blessing to me and such a bane to my wife.

The largest section by far is filled with Bible commentaries. When preparing a Bible study, I have looked up all relevant writers, but only after I have prepared as much as I can on my own. Then I have both added to and corrected my efforts in the light of scholarly and devotional writings.

It would be impossible to name all those to whom I have been indebted. Like many others I devoured William Barclay's *Daily Bible Readings* as soon as they were issued back in the 1950s. His knowledge of New Testament background and vocabulary was invaluable and his simple and clear style a model to follow, though I later came to question his 'liberal' interpretations. John Stott, Merill Tenney, Gordon Fee and William Hendrickson were among those who opened up the New Testament for me, while Alec Motyer, G. T. Wenham and Derek Kidner did the same for the Old. And time would fail to tell of Denney, Lightfoot, Nygren, Robinson, Adam Smith, Howard, Ellison, Mullen, Ladd, Atkinson, Green, Beasley-Murray, Snaith, Marshall, Morris, Pink and many many others. Nor must I forget two remarkable little books from the pens of women: *What the Bible is all about* by Henrietta Mears and *Christ in all the Scriptures* by A. M. Hodgkin. To have sat at their feet has been an inestimable privilege. I have always regarded a willingness to learn as one of the fundamental qualifications to be a teacher.

I soaked up all these sources like a sponge. I remembered so much of *what* I read, but could not easily recall *where* I had read it. This did not seem to matter too much when gathering material for preaching, since most of these writers were precisely aiming to help preachers and did not expect to be constantly quoted. Indeed, a sermon full of attributed quotations can be distracting, if not misinterpreted as name-dropping or indirectly claiming to be well read. As could my previous paragraph!

But printing, unlike preaching, is subject to copyright, since royalties are involved. And the fear of breaching this held me back from allowing any of my spoken ministry to be reproduced in print. It would be out of the question to trace back 40 years' scrounging and even if that were possible, the necessary footnotes and acknowledgements could double the size and price of these volumes.

The alternative was to deny access to my material for those who could most benefit from it, which my publisher persuaded me would be wrong. At least I was responsible for collecting and collating it all, but I dare to believe that there is sufficient original contribution to justify its release.

I can only offer an apology and my gratitude to all those whose studies I have plundered over the years, whether in small or large amounts, hoping they might see this as an example of that imitation which is the sincerest form of flattery. To use another quotation I read somewhere: 'Certain authors, speaking of their works, say "my book" … They would do better to say "our book" … because there is in them usually more of other people's than their own' (the original came from Pascal).

So here is 'our' book! I suppose I am what the French bluntly call a 'vulgarizer'. That is someone who takes what the academics teach and makes it simple enough for the 'common' people to understand. I am content with that. As one old lady said to me, after I had expounded a quite profound passage of Scripture, 'You broke it up small enough for us to take it in.' I have, in fact, always aimed so to teach that a 12-year-old boy could understand and remember my message.

Some readers will be disappointed, even frustrated, with the paucity of text references, especially if they want to check me out! But their absence is intentional. God gave us his Word in books, but not in chapters and verses. That was the work of two bishops, French and Irish, centuries later. It became easier to find a 'text' and to ignore context. How many Christians who quote John 3:16 can recite verses 15 and 17? Many no longer 'search the scriptures'; they simply look them up (given the numbers). So I have followed the apostles' habit of naming the authors only – 'as Isaiah or David or Samuel said'. For example, the Bible says that God whistles. Where on earth does it say that? In the book of Isaiah. Whereabouts? Go and find out for yourself. Then you'll also find out when he did and why he did. And you'll have the satisfaction of having discovered all that by yourself.

One final word. Behind my hope that these introductions to the Bible books will help you to get to know and love them more than you did lies a much greater and deeper longing – that you will also come to know better and love more the subject of all the books, the Lord Himself. I was deeply touched by the remark of someone who had watched all the videos within a matter of days: 'I know so much more about the Bible now, but the biggest thing was that I felt the heart of God as never before.'

What more could a Bible teacher ask? May you experience the same as you read these pages and join me in saying: Praise Father, Son and Holy Spirit.

J. David Pawson
Sherborne St John, 2000

Yes, I thought I knew my Bible,
Reading piecemeal, hit or miss:
Now a part of John or Matthew,
Then a bit of Genesis.

Certain chapters of Isaiah,
Certain psalms, the twenty-third,
First of Proverbs, twelfth of Romans –
Yes, I thought I knew the Word.

But I found that thorough reading
Was a different thing to do
And the way was unfamiliar
When I read my Bible through.

You who like to play at Bible,
Dip and dabble here and there,
Just before you kneel all weary,
Yawning through a hurried prayer.

You who treat this crown of writings
As you treat no other book:
Just a paragraph disjointed,
Just a crude impatient look.

Try a worthier procedure,
Try a broad and steady view;
You will kneel in awesome wonder
When you read the Bible through.

Author unknown

# INTRODUCTION
TO PROPHECY

This volume focuses on the pre-exilic prophets – that is, prophets whose ministry came before the two exiles of God's people. The people of the northern kingdom (Israel) were deported to Assyria in 722 BC and those of the southern kingdom (Judah) were led off to Babylon in 587 BC. Most of the prophets in this volume are concerned with warning the people that God would send them into exile if they did not return to the covenant. Such a disaster seemed inconceivable, for the people could not imagine that God would let his Temple be destroyed and his people removed from the land he had promised them.

This was not the only focus of the prophets' message. Some also had things to say to the nations surrounding Israel and Judah, and some were given messages exclusively directed to another nation.

There is much confusion regarding the nature of prophecy both in the Bible and today, so a few words of explanation are needed before we examine the books themselves.

Prophecy had been part of the life of the people of God from their beginning as a nation. Moses was described as a prophet, and the Old Testament books that we think of as history in our Bibles are called prophetic books in the Jewish Scriptures. The pre-exilic prophets begin what are known as the 'book prophets' (i.e. whole Bible books consisting solely of one prophet's message, whereas the 'earlier prophets' were embedded in historical narratives, often more than one in each), though their order in the Bible does not reflect the order in which the books were written.

They were very ordinary men, but they had the very extraordinary function of speaking for God. They received their messages from God in both words and pictures. The words became 'heavy within them', so that they felt a burden which was only eased when it was passed on.

The 'pictures' were called visions when they came while the prophet was awake, and dreams if they came during sleep. It is important to realize when reading prophecy that when the prophets describe their visions they usually do so in the past tense, as if the things they have seen have already happened. We would put it in the future tense and say, 'I have seen what is going to happen', but the prophet either puts it in the present tense – 'I see it happening' – or in the past tense – 'I have seen it happening'. In both cases, the prophecy predicts the future. The descriptions are very detailed. Nahum, for example, actually saw the red uniforms of the soldiers who would destroy Babylon. No known enemy in Nahum's time wore red, but the Persians, newly on the scene, destroyed Babylon wearing red coats.

The prophetic gifting had two sides to it. The ability to speak for God depended on the ability to hear from God. The message had to be received before it could be given. It came to the prophet through different channels, physical, mental or spiritual.

God may speak in an audible voice. God is not often recorded as doing this in the Bible – when he did, many people thought it was thunder – as, for example, when he said to Jesus at his baptism, 'You are my beloved son.'

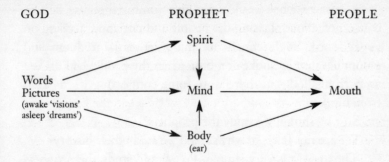

God can also put words into the mind so that the prophet knows he is hearing God's voice. Over time the prophet will learn to distinguish thoughts implanted by God from those of his own mind.

Also, God can speak to the prophet's spirit and implant words or impressions that his mind doesn't understand. For example, when someone prays in tongues, God speaks to the person's spirit and puts words into their mouth, although their mind doesn't understand what has happened.

Of course, God can also speak to the body and then straight to the mouth, bypassing mind and spirit altogether – as he did with Balaam's ass in the Book of Numbers. But this is very rare.

Regardless of the means of reception, words from God must ultimately come out of the prophet's mouth and be delivered to the people.

Two categories of message were common: messages of challenge, when people were sinning, and messages of comfort, when they were doing right. If the messages generally seem more negative, this is because God usually needed to speak when there were problems. So many of the prophetical messages are challenge rather than comfort. In the Book of Isaiah the first half is challenge and the second half is comfort.

A false prophet would only give comfort because he was concerned about pleasing the people and not about passing on God's word. So Jeremiah became a byword for doom and gloom because he spoke at a time when the people had drifted away from God (but there were some comforting words even from him).

So why should we study the prophets?

We are not Jews, so why should we study their history?

The answer is very simple. We should study the prophets so that we may get to know God better, because God has not changed. The prophets reveal God – the God who revealed himself as the great 'I am' or 'Always'.

There are three major things that the prophets seem to focus on, as the chart shows:

1. God's activity – powerful
Nature: miracles
History: movements

2. God's integrity – predictable
Justice: punishment
Mercy: pardon

3. God's flexibility – personal
Man: repents
God: relents

1. The prophets focus on the activity of God – what he has done, what he is doing, what he is going to do. When we recite the Apostles' Creed in church, we begin with the words, 'I believe in God the Father Almighty, Maker of heaven and earth.' That is how the prophets present him – as a God who is so powerful that he is in total control of both nature and

history. Therefore he can make miracles happen in nature and he can cause movements to happen in history. This is a concept of God that we must keep hold of in our modern, scientific age, in which most people regard nature as a closed system and history as the result of economic forces. It is not easy to remember that God is in total control of both nature and history. Reading the prophets regularly keeps in our minds this picture of a mighty God who can make anything happen in nature and history.

2. The prophets focus on God's integrity – they show us that God is consistent. He is always the same; he does not change in character. He is a unique combination of justice and mercy. If you stress one more than the other, you will get an unbalanced view of God. If you only think of God's justice, you get too hard a view of God. If you only think of his mercy, you get too soft a view of him. In the one case there will be fear but no love, and in the other case there will be love but no fear. The prophets provide a wonderful balance. God's justice means that he must punish sin, and his mercy means that he longs to forgive it and pardon it. This tension for God is only resolved at the cross, because only at the cross do justice and mercy meet. Sins are both punished and pardoned at the same place and at the same time – Jesus takes the punishment and we get the pardon. The integrity of God's character means that you can predict how God will behave. He will exercise mercy as long as he can, but when it is persistently refused he must exercise justice. That's the message of Jonah and Nahum, for example.

3. The prophets emphasize God's flexibility. I believe this is a most important insight into God's character. He can change his plans – they are not fixed for all eternity, but they change depending on how people respond to him. This is especially seen in a section of the prophecy of Jeremiah, where the prophet went to the potter's house and saw the potter trying to

make the clay into a beautiful vase. But the clay would not run well in the potter's hands to make this vase, so the potter pushed it back into a lump and made a crude, thick pot with it. God said to Jeremiah, 'Have you learned the lesson of the potter and the clay?' Most of the preachers I've heard preach on this passage misunderstand it. They say that the potter decides what shape the clay will be and that this implies predestination – if God decides your destiny, you are stuck with it. Actually the clay decides whether to be a beautiful vase or a crude pot, for it decides on whether it responds to the potter's hands. God said he wanted to make Israel a vessel of his mercy, but they wouldn't have it, so he made them a pot full of his justice.

So the prophets speak of a God who is personal, who is alive and who calls us into a living relationship with him. Things are not fixed – that's fatalism. God is flexible – he adjusts to his people. Where his people respond rightly, he makes us into a beautiful vessel. But when we respond wrongly, he will still make a vessel of us, but it will be a vessel full of his justice, and we will be a demonstration of God's justice to the rest of the world. The choice is ours. What sort of clay do we want to be? Do we want to demonstrate his mercy to the world or his justice?

The flexibility of God is a very precious truth to me, but sadly, it's a picture of God that most Christians have not grasped. The future is not fixed; it's not predetermined; it's open, because God is personal. The one thing that God cannot change is the past, but he can and will change the future. The Bible even dares to say that God repents when we repent. This need not alarm us. The word 'repent' simply means 'to change one's mind'. So when we change our mind, God changes his! But he doesn't change his character, so we can always rely on him.

So it is a good thing to read the prophets and get to know God better. He is a powerful God and can do anything in nature and history. He's a predictable God – he will act according to his integrity of character – and therefore we can know how he will respond. But he is also a personal God who wants a living relationship with us so that he can respond to us and we can respond to him. That's the God we worship.

The pre-exilic prophets include some of the best and least known of the prophets, but together they give us a good range of the style and focus of prophetic ministry.

PART I

JONAH

Introduction

This introduction to Jonah encompasses Nahum as well, for there were significant similarities between these two prophets. Jonah and Nahum both went to the same place and they both had the same sort of message.

Jonah was born near Nazareth. He was a local hero to the people of Nazareth, and Jesus must have heard about him when he was a little boy. Of all the prophets, Jesus compared himself to Jonah.

Nahum came from Capernaum. *Caper* means 'village', so *Caper-Nahum* is named after the prophet. This village was Jesus' main base on the Sea of Galilee, so he had a very close connection with these two prophets.

It is especially significant that they came from the north, because this was the international part of Israel. It was called 'Galilee of the nations' because the crossroads of the world was in Galilee. A road from Europe came down the coast and crossed through the region before heading east to Arabia. The road from Africa came up from Egypt and crossed through Galilee and north to Damascus. So everyone going from Asia to Africa or from Europe to Arabia came through this crossroads. At the crossroads there was a little hill called Megiddo. 'The Hill of Megiddo' in Hebrew is 'Armageddon', where the last battle of history will be fought. So Nazareth was on a hill overlooking the crossroads. As a boy Jesus must have seen many coming and going, rather like travellers passing through an airport lounge.

Galilee was very international, whereas up in the hills of Judea in the south the people were nationalistic, isolated and right off the main routes.

So there were two locations within the nation which affected the ministry of Jesus. He was very popular in the international place in the north, but he was very unpopular in the nationalist centre in the south, where he was eventually crucified.

Jonah and Nahum were northerners and were therefore very much aware of international affairs, and they were both sent by God to Assyria.

The threats to the Holy Land came from the big western and eastern powers. Israel was continually being squeezed between these two power blocs as each tried to overcome the other. Somebody has said about Israel that if you live in the middle of a crossroads you're bound to get run over, and that's exactly what happened. In the days of Jonah and Nahum, Assyria, with its capital at Nineveh, was the problem.

Jonah went to challenge Assyria in 770 BC and Nahum went in 620 BC, so they were 150 years apart. They were both sent because of the sheer wickedness of the Assyrian people. The Assyrian empire lasted for about 750 years and at one stage even managed to take over Egypt. It started as a small power in about 1354 BC and gradually expanded. But it expanded by means of great cruelty. Indeed, the Assyrians were one of the most cruel, brutal nations that history has seen. They invented the hideous practice of impaling their enemies on wooden spikes until they died. They used to execute thousands of people at once in this way. They ruled their empire by terror.

Nahum called the capital Nineveh a 'bloody city', and the name was well deserved. If a nation thought that the Assyrians had their eye on their country they were mortally afraid of what would happen.

Zephaniah also spoke about the Assyrians, but Nahum finally went to them and said, 'You're finished! God's going to wipe you out.' And, sure enough, Nineveh fell in 612 BC, and the whole Assyrian empire disappeared five years later, immediately after Nahum's warning.

Fact or fiction?

Turning to the story of Jonah itself, we must first respond to the huge debate about whether it is fact or fiction. Most people know the book because of the story of 'Jonah and the whale' and most people's impressions of the book depend on whether or not they believe that the story is true.

Some say that the incident in which the whale (or big fish) swallows Jonah is like the story of Pinocchio, who also lived inside a whale. They argue that no one could be expected to take such a fantastic story seriously. Therefore they take it to be a parable with a moral and offer various options as to the meaning. Some say it was told to challenge the hearers to greater missionary endeavour – it was a reminder to Israel that they had a missionary responsibility to the rest of the world. Jonah's running away from his mission is a moral for Israel to learn from.

But when there is a parable in the Bible, it is usually very clearly indicated. Jonah, however, is treated as history. Also, when Jesus told parables they never contained miracles, and yet there are eight miracles in this story.

Other scholars believe that the Book of Jonah is an allegory, with every incident corresponding to real life. So Jonah is a personification of Israel, rather as John Bull is of Britain or Uncle Sam is of the United States. They say that Jonah being swallowed by the whale is a metaphorical picture of Israel being swallowed up in exile.

But there are serious objections to treating Jonah as fiction.

1 The style of the book is exactly the same as all the historical books. Its wording, style and grammar are identical to those of 1 and 2 Kings.

2 The book deals with real places and real people mentioned elsewhere in the Bible. Jonah is mentioned in 2 Kings, and so we know that he was a prophet during the reign of Jeroboam II. His father was Anatai and he is treated as a real person in the historical books of the Bible.

3 More importantly, Jesus treated Jonah as a real person. He believed in Jonah and the big fish. Jesus said of himself that 'a greater than Jonah is now here', and he likened his own period of death to Jonah's time in the whale.

4 But above all, the theories claiming that Jonah is a parable or an allegory do not do justice to chapter 4. The main question that opens up the message of the book is 'Why did Jonah run away?' Many people never even bother to ask the question! Why, then, are people so eager to treat Jonah as the man who never was? Why are they so reluctant to accept this book as fact?

The first objection is that what happened to him was physically impossible. The second is that it was psychologically improbable that one Jewish preacher could convert a huge pagan city. Could we imagine a Jew arriving in the middle of London, preaching in Trafalgar Square and bringing the city back to God? It seems very unlikely that the whole of London would repent.

As for the physical impossibility, we must first ask, 'Could it happen?' Secondly, we must ask, 'Could God make it happen?'

Is it possible for a man to be swallowed by a great fish or whale?

When I was a pastor in the village of Chalfont St Peter, Buckinghamshire, the local blacksmith had a son who worked with marine mammals in California. He trained a whale and a dolphin who were friends and played together in a large tank. When the dolphin died the whale wouldn't allow the keepers to touch the body of his dead friend, and kept the body of the dolphin in its mouth for three days. It would periodically bring the dolphin above the water to try to get it to breathe again. The blacksmith's son showed us a film he had taken of these three days, and the dolphin was just about the size of a man.

This incident links with an unusual newspaper story about a whaler named James Bartley who was working off the Falkland Islands. He and three other men were thrown into the sea when a whale came up under their boat. The other men were rescued, but not Bartley. The captain wrote in his log, 'Swept overboard, presumed drowned, James Bartley.'

Later they happened to catch the whale that had capsized the boat. As they were cutting it up they saw something moving inside the whale's belly. They cut it open to find James Bartley in a deep coma. But it was clear that he was still breathing. After a few days he recovered consciousness and went on to live a normal life. His only handicap was that where his skin had not been covered by clothing, it had been bleached by the digestive juices of the whale, so he had a very unusual appearance for the rest of his life. So this true story proves that it is physically possible to survive within the belly of a whale.

Some Christians seem eager to believe anything. A Salvation Army officer once said that if the Bible said that

Jonah swallowed the whale he'd believe it! But this kind of blind faith just draws ridicule from the world. All things are possible with God, but the Bible doesn't ask you to believe the absurd.

DEAD OR ALIVE?

The key question for me is whether Jonah was dead or alive.

I had never asked myself that question until I saw the film of the whale with the dolphin in its mouth trying to get it to breathe again. But when I re-read the Book of Jonah, to my astonishment I found that all the evidence points to the fact that the whale picked up a dead body.

If you read chapter 2 you discover that Jonah was actually drowned. We read that when the sailors threw him into the sea he sank to the bed of the bottom and lay there at the roots of the mountains, with his head in the seaweed. It takes only about a minute and a half to drown, and it takes much longer than that to reach the bottom of the sea! Sunday school materials mistakenly picture the whale floating around on the surface with its mouth open when the sailors threw him overboard. None picture him, as the Bible does, lying in the seaweed at the bottom of the Mediterranean.

Furthermore, the prayer which he prays tells us that he is in Sheol, the abode of the dead. He describes his last moment of consciousness, when his life was ebbing away and the waters engulfed him. He says that at that time he remembered the Lord.

So as all the evidence points to Jonah having died. It seems that the whale does not lead to Jonah's survival but to his resurrection. When the whale spewed him up, God reunited his spirit and body. This ties in with Jesus' statement that, just as Jonah was in the belly of the whale, so he would be in the heart of the earth.

Worldly sceptics would find it easier to believe that Jonah was swallowed and remained alive in the whale than the idea that he died and was resurrected! I believe that Jonah is the most outstanding example of resurrection in the Old Testament.

MIRACLES

The interpretation of the Book of Jonah leads us to face bigger questions about our belief in God. In this book it is not just the swallowing of Jonah by a whale that we have to come to terms with, but a total of eight physical miracles, including a far bigger miracle than the one that most people associate with the book.

For in the last chapter God tells a worm to do something. The blacksmith's son in California could train whales quite easily – they are highly intelligent mammals – but I've never seen anyone train a worm! But God tells a worm what to do. If anybody says to me, 'You don't still believe that story about Jonah and the whale, do you?' I say, 'That's nothing – I believe the story about the worm too!' They usually look quite blank because they have no idea what I'm talking about.

Let us briefly consider the miracles in this book:

1 God sends a wind that causes a storm, and the ship is in danger.
2 When the sailors cast lots to find out who is the cause of divine anger, they identify Jonah. God has controlled the outcome of an apparently random selection.
3 When the sailors throw Jonah overboard, God calms the sea.
4 God sends the great fish to swallow Jonah's body.
5 God makes the great fish vomit the body on to dry land.
6 God makes a vine (a castor plant, from which we get castor oil) grow overnight.

7 God sends a worm to eat the roots of the plant so that it
  dies.
8 Finally God sends a hot, scorching desert wind.

So on eight occasions God controls nature.

How we react to these events tells us a lot. There are three
philosophies that are widely held in the UK:

1 *Atheism* says that God didn't create the world and therefore
  he doesn't control it.
2 *Deism* is a more common philosophy which holds that God
  created the world but that he can't control it now. I would
  say that many people in British churches are Deists, which
  means that they can't believe in miracles. So they go to
  church and thank God that he is the Maker of heaven and
  earth, but they won't pray about the weather!
3 *Theism* is the biblical philosophy which says that God
  not only created the world in the past but also controls
  it now.

Of course, there are some Christians who combine two of
these philosophies. They believe in miracles in the Bible but
they don't believe that they happen today. They are practical
deists and theoretical theists.

Converting Nineveh

Let us turn next to the psychological improbability that an
enormous city like Nineveh would convert. Here are some
arguments in favour of this being an historical fact:

1 First, they were religious and even superstitious. They
  actually believed in God.

2 Secondly, they were guilty. Guilt makes cowards of us all, so when they were accused of what they had done, they knew it and were prepared to own up.

3 Thirdly, the revival started at the bottom among the ordinary people and worked its way up to the palace.

4 Fourthly, they had the sign of Jonah. If Jonah's skin was white from his time in the whale, he must have been quite a sight. No doubt his explanation of what had happened to him made a big impression on them.

5 Fifthly, above all, when the Holy Spirit works, things happen.

I don't have any difficulty in believing that the whole city repented. Jesus certainly believed it when he said that the people of Nineveh will rise up on the Day of Judgement, because they repented when they heard about God and his hearers did not.

Why did Jonah run away?

But there is a big question that we have not yet considered in detail. Why did Jonah run away from his task? This is the subject of chapter 4, which is rarely taught, preached or even read. Yet it is the very heart of this little story. Why was Jonah so reluctant? Who was he thinking about?

Some people say he was thinking primarily of himself. He was just scared to go to Nineveh – he feared being impaled as an enemy of Assyria. But this doesn't explain why he suggested that the sailors throw him into the sea. He wasn't afraid of death as such.

Secondly, people say he thought that the Gentiles had no right to hear about the God of Israel. It was a kind of reverse of anti-Semitism – we might call it 'anti-Gentilism'. But this doesn't explain why he fled away to the Gentiles in Tarsus.

Others say that he was thinking of the Assyrians, the wickedest people on earth. And yet, more than that, he was really thinking of Israel, because Assyria was the biggest threat to little Israel, and he didn't want to have anything to do with this potential invader.

None of these solutions take into account the words of Jonah in the last chapter. He had told the people of Nineveh that in 40 days God would wipe out their city. The result of his preaching was that the people all repented. Disaster was averted.

An evangelist would be thrilled if a whole city repented, but Jonah was disappointed. He sat on a hill outside the town and said to God, 'I told you this would happen! I know what you're like. I knew you'd let them off. I knew you would just threaten them with destruction, but then fail to go through with it!' Doesn't Jonah want people to be saved? Is he so narrow-minded and so bigoted that he doesn't want people to repent?

The key is his reference to what he had said to God in his own country: 'O Lord, is this not what I said when I was still at home? That is why I was so quick to flee to Tarshish. I knew that you are a gracious and compassionate God, slow to anger and abounding in love, a God who relents from sending calamity' (4:2).

We must look to 2 Kings 14:23–25 to find out what had happened to Jonah in his own land.

When he was called to be a prophet he was sent to the King Jeroboam II of Israel – a notoriously bad king who did evil in the sight of the Lord. When God told Jonah to go to the king, Jonah responded positively at first, expecting to be able to deal with the king's wickedness. But the message that Jonah was given was not what he had expected. The Lord said, 'Go and tell the king that I want to bless him, that I'm going to enlarge his borders and make him great.' Jonah protested that he was a wicked king and that this was the wrong approach.

He was saying to the Lord in his heart, 'It'll never work, Lord. If you bless bad people they just get worse.'

Indeed, the king did get worse. The more the Lord blessed him, the worse he got. So Jonah came to the conclusion that mercy doesn't change wicked people. Jonah is telling God that he knows God's business better than God himself does.

God's compassion

So this past episode coloured Jonah's attitude as he went to Nineveh. He said, 'Let's just see what happens, Lord. I'm going to watch this city and see whether your letting them off will cure them or not, whether they get better or worse.'

Underlying all this is Jonah's jealousy for the Lord's character and reputation. He could not cope with anyone taking advantage of divine mercy. He believed their repentance was superficial and would not last. He thought that if God was too soft with them, they would conclude that he never carries out his threats of judgement. Jonah's warning would be doubted, even ridiculed, and eventually forgotten.

When the plant grew up alongside him, he was very thankful for it, since it gave him shade from the sun. But when the worm ate the roots it died, and Jonah was very angry again. He asked God why he had caused it to die. God told Jonah that it was legitimate for him to be angry about the plant, but did he have a right to be angry about Nineveh? There were over 120,000 children in the city and many cattle too. Didn't God have a right to have a heart for them?

So although Jonah was jealous for the Lord in not wanting to see the Assyrians escape punishment, he did not understand God's compassion, his desire to postpone punishment as long as possible. That was why he ran away to sea, and that was why, for him, the success of his preaching was so hollow. We too sometimes forget how patient God is and how full of mercy he is and how many chances he wants to give people.

There is a time, of course, when God's patience runs out. This is ultimately the message of the prophets – Jonah just got the timing wrong. In his day it was still the time of God's mercy and patience with Nineveh. But that patience would not last for ever, as we shall see when we study the prophecy of Nahum.

PART II

JOEL

Introduction

We know nothing about Joel except his name and the name of his father, Pethuel. As both names contain the Hebrew word *el* ('God'), we may assume that they were from a godly family, but we can say little about them with any certainty.

Joel's prophecy was given 10 years after Obadiah's. The prophecy of Obadiah was almost exclusively directed at other nations and held out a prospect of good things for Israel. Joel, however, picked up on the concept of the 'Day of the Lord', which Obadiah had used, but said that judgement would fall not only on 'the nations' but on Israel too. This came as a considerable shock to the people of Israel, who assumed that they were all right in the sight of God.

Similarly, many Christian people today complacently assume that they will safely arrive in heaven, however they live. In fact, sin among God's people is more serious than sin outside of God's people. In Romans 2 Paul reminds his readers that if they do the same things that they criticize unbelievers for, they will not escape the wrath of God. God has no favourites. The idea that once you belong to God you can sin freely is totally unbiblical. He has not given a blank chequebook for us to use whenever we sin. It would be totally unfair of God to condemn an unbeliever to hell for adultery but, in the case of a believer guilty of the same behaviour, to say, 'Here is your ticket to heaven.'

So the prophets had to correct that idea in Israel first, because the people of Israel thought they were all right. Elijah had challenged them strongly, but Joel was the first to say that the Day of the Lord could bring darkness, not light.

I find it helpful to analyse the whole Book of Joel before intererpreting it. The three chapters coincide with the three sections of the prophecy, though we are not told if they were delivered separately or all at once.

An outline of the Book of Joel

The plague of locusts (chapter 1)
The ruin of the land (1:1–12)
The repentance of the people (1:13–20)

The Day of the Lord (chapter 2)
A terrible repetition (2:1–11)
A true repentance (2:12–17)
A timeless recovery (2:18–27)
A total restoration (2:28–32)
   (a) Spirit, men and women (2:28–29)
   (b) Signs, sun and moon (2:30–31)
   (c) Salvation, calling and called (2:32)

The Valley of Decision (chapter 3)
Vengeance on the nations (3:1–16a)
Vindication of Israel (3:16b–21)

The plague of locusts (chapter 1)

The ruin of the land (1:1–12)

The prophecy of Joel was sparked off by a natural disaster. A plague of locusts had hit the country. It must have been an extraordinary sight. Locusts are like big grasshoppers. In a swarm of locusts there may be up to 600 million insects covering 400 square miles. They can eat up to 80,000 tons of food a day, so when they descend on an area all vegetation disappears. They travel 2,000 miles per month at a speed of between 2 and 10 miles per day for 6 weeks and lay 5,000 eggs per square foot. Their appetite is voracious and their heads look like those of horses.

My only experience of them was in Kano in northern Nigeria. Although it was midday, it suddenly became dark. I thought it was an eclipse of the sun until I saw a huge black cloud approaching that had blotted out the sun, and soon we were in darkness as if it were midnight. I estimated that the locusts were moving at 12 miles per hour, and it took an hour and a half for them to pass. After they had passed we saw that the trees had been stripped of their bark as well as their leaves. Every living piece of vegetation was destroyed. I will never forget it. It was an horrific experience.

Although they are common in Africa, swarms of locusts are comparatively rare in Israel. So when they arrived, Joel told the people that God was behind it. He told them that it was the first of God's warnings that if they continued living as they were, something even worse would happen.

As a result of the locusts the people didn't have enough grain to make a grain offering in the Temple. Public worship ceased. The vineyards, orchards and olive groves had all been destroyed. The nation faced drought, bush fires and starvation, and the economy was at a complete standstill. Some have speculated that Joel's message was given at the Jewish harvest festival known as the Feast of Tabernacles – the very time when they should have been celebrating the harvest of their crops.

There was biblical precedent for understanding the plague as God's judgement. In Exodus 10 the eighth plague (of locusts) in Egypt was sent by God, and in Deteronomy 28 God said he would send plagues if the people were disobedient.

This raises an interesting question for us today: How do we know when a disaster is from God?

We should look for three things:

1 it is directed against his people;
2 it has been prophesied beforehand;
3 it is unusual in either its scale or its detail.

So, to use a fairly recent example, I believe that the fire in York Minster was an example of God at work. It is its unusual character that convinces me in particular. The lightning that struck York Minster came from a small cloud that circled York Minster for 20 minutes in a blue sky. The cloud wasn't big enough for rain, yet it discharged a lightning bolt (without any thunder) that burnt the cathedral from the top down, just after they had renovated it and installed the latest smoke-detection and fire-fighting equipment. Choir boys marching through the cathedral saw it happen, but they heard nothing because there was no thunder at all. I obtained a map of that cloud from the Meteorological Office, and 16 non-Christian meteorologists said that it had to be from God. It was the most unusual thing they had seen in a long time.

People asked me if it was God's judgement. I said I believed it was God's mercy. He waited until everybody had left the cathedral after that degrading consecration of a bishop who denied the faith. He could have done it while they were all still in there. So I believe that the incident expressed his mercy rather than his judgement, but I also believe it was a warning.

So one of the signs that an event is from God is its unusual nature. The unnatural often demonstrates the supernatural. Another sign is the discernment of God's people, and there were many people with prophetic gifts who saw God's hand in the York Minster disaster. Although none had prophesied beforehand, many wondered what God might do if a bishop were consecrated with such errant beliefs.

But disasters, whether they are direct from God or not, are always a reminder of God's judgement. It is important to realize this, lest we make inappropriate assessments about everything that takes place. In Luke 13 Jesus is asked to comment upon the tragic deaths of some labourers when the Tower of Siloam fell down. He is asked if they were greater sinners than anybody else. Jesus replies that they weren't, but unless those who saw the disaster repent of their sin, they too will perish. Every earthquake, typhoon and flood is a reminder to us of the frailty of life and the need to get right with God.

The repentance of the people (1:13–20)

In the second half of chapter 1 Joel tells the elders to call for a national act of repentance, warning them that if they do not repent there will be a terrible repetition of God's judgement, though he is not specific about what they should repent of. We are left to research the historical background in 1 and 2 Kings to find out what was happening at the time which required that the nation should receive such a warning.

We cannot be definite about the period when Joel prophesied, but it was probably during the ninth century BC, which may tie in with particular events in 1 and 2 Kings. A clue may be the fact that there is a reference to the priests in Joel, but no reference to a king. In the books of Kings there is a period when there is a queen on the throne (841–835 BC) – the only time in the history of God's people when this was the case. God had promised King David that as long as the kings kept the statutes and commands of God, they would never lack a son to sit on the throne of Israel. He allowed them to have a king, but not a queen.

Furthermore, the female monarch in question was Queen Athaliah, who had behaved treacherously. She had been the queen mother, and when the king died she seized the throne and murdered all of his sons, so that she could be queen. Her mother was the infamous Jezebel, who had wrought havoc in the northern kingdom. But one son of the king was saved by the High Priest and hidden in the Temple. Had she managed to kill every boy, the royal line of David would have ended. But despite her despicable behaviour, the people accepted her as their ruler. Even the High Priest didn't object – though at least he had the courage to hide the boy. The boy's name was Joash, and shortly after Joel had preached, the people gained the courage to depose Athaliah and put Joash on the throne, even though he was only seven years old.

So Joel's prophecy was possibly given against this background. National sin had been committed and therefore national repentance was required.

The Day of the Lord (chapter 2)

A terrible repetition (2:1–11)

But the people did not repent. They continued to sin, so at the beginning of chapter 2 Joel describes what is at first sight a repetition of the plague of locusts. But when you look at the text more closely it becomes clear that this time this plague of

locusts is actually just a picture of thousands of soldiers marching into the land and destroying everything, rather as locusts
would. It is a far more alarming picture than even the first one.
Indeed, given the total destruction, it is very likely that Joel
was describing the Babylonians, who, alone among all the
ancient peoples who conquered others, had a terrible scorched-
earth policy. They not only killed all the people and their
children, but also destroyed every living thing, including trees,
sheep and cattle. The Babylonian army left nothing alive, and
that is a very similar picture to a locust plague. There are parallels here with Revelation 9, where, once again, a plague of
locusts is described followed by an army from the East of 200
million soldiers. Whether Joel is describing soldiers or another
plague of locusts, it is clear that God was capable of sending
both and that his judgement was still necessary.

A true repentance (2:12–17)

Again Joel repeats the message that what God is looking for is
true repentance. After his first call for repentance most of the
people just went out and got drunk. People have twofold reactions to coming disaster. Some prepare and repent, others get
drunk.

So Joel issues a second call for true repentance. One of the
memorable phrases in this second call is 'Rend your hearts and
not your garments.' Watching someone tear their clothes can
be impressive, but that isn't good enough for God. It is our
hearts that matter, not what we do to our clothes. It is interesting to note that Joel does not list the sins. We can only assume
that the people were only too aware of what God was concerned about.

We do well to remember that God says he is willing to
change his mind concerning their punishment. They are in a
dynamic relationship with God – he will respond to them. So

God tells them how to pray: they must plead for mercy and call on God to demonstrate his love and faithfulness to them as his people in the land he has given them.

A timeless recovery (2:18–27)

Some speculate that this part of the prophecy was not given at the same time as the earlier parts. Here Joel urges the people to be glad rather than afraid. He promises Israel that if they really repent from their hearts, God will restore the years that the locusts have eaten. This is a principle that applies today. Many regret the wasted years in their lives, but God says he will restore those years to them. But he will only restore the years that the locusts have eaten if there is true repentance.

The root of repentance is that we 'change our minds'. So it is appropriate to say that if they repent, God will change his mind. God assures them three times that never again will he act in this way, and that then they will know him.

A total restoration (2:28–32)

Joel moves on to some wonderful promises. God says that if they truly repent, never again will he punish them with such action. Instead, there will be a total restoration – not just a physical restoration of the crops that the locusts ate, but also a spiritual restoration.

(A) SPIRIT, MEN AND WOMEN (2:28–29)

One of the greatest promises given in the Book of Joel is that God will pour out his Spirit on all kinds of people, regardless of sex, class or age. Young men will see visions and old men will dream dreams. Also, maidservants and menservants will prophesy. God promises to put his prophetic Spirit in all kinds of people. This promise was picked up by the apostle Peter on the Day of Pentecost eight centuries later. He explained that

Joel's prophecy was coming true as the Spirit came upon the 120 disciples.

(B) SIGNS, SUN AND MOON (2:30-31)

The second part of the promise is that the sun will be darkened and the moon will be turned to blood. Some say this was fulfilled when Jesus died and the sun was darkened for three hours, but this sign actually remains to be fulfilled at the end of the age, for Jesus himself mentions it as a sign of his second coming in Matthew 24:29.

It is interesting that there will be signs in the sky, because the sky responds to significant events on earth. People foolishly tell me that the fact that the Wise Men followed the star proves that astrology is all right. But I tell them that they have got it totally wrong. Astrology believes that the position of the stars influences a baby at the moment of birth, but at Bethlehem it was the position of the baby that influenced the stars! So when Jesus died the sun went out. The universe responds to significant events down here. That's amazing, isn't it? We are not governed by the stars; they are governed by God.

(C) SALVATION, CALLING AND CALLED (2:32)

Joel also promised salvation for everyone whom the Lord called and who responded to the Lord. Salvation was not automatic, as if the nation as a whole was 'saved' through some mystical process. There is a double call in salvation. God calls people to be saved, through human preachers, and people in turn call on God.

I don't like telling people to repeat the sinner's prayer – I just tell them to call on the Lord themselves. We are told that 'Whoever calls on the name of the Lord shall be saved.' It is very important that people themselves should call on his name.

Whoever does that will be saved. Peter picked that up at Pentecost, and 3,000 people called on the name of the Lord and were saved that day.

So Joel's promise of total restoration is not just about crops, wine and corn, but about human hearts.

Joel said that all this would happen on the Day of the Lord. We don't need to believe that it is literally a day of 24 hours; the word 'day' is flexible in Scripture. The Hebrew word *yom* can mean a whole epoch. If I say, 'The day of the horse and cart is over', I don't mean a period of 24 hours. I mean that an historical era is finished and we are in the day of the motor car. That is the meaning of the word 'day' in 'the Day of the Lord'. The point is this: man has had his day, and the devil has had his day, but one day God is going to have his day. There is coming the Day of the Lord when he will have his say, when he will bring the world under his rule.

Joel mentions the Day of the Lord five times in his prophecy, always referring to it as a time of judgement. The phrase is also picked up by later prophets such as Isaiah, Jeremiah, Ezekiel, Amos, Zephaniah and Malachi. The Day of the Lord is also a prominent part of the New Testament (see 1 Corinthians, 1 Thessalonians, 2 Thessalonians and 2 Peter). There is a day coming when the Lord will have his day, and that will be the last day.

So the order of judgement is: first, God's people, and then his enemies later. We have a choice: do we want judgement now or later?

We are now in the 'last days', which began when Joel's prophecy came true and the Spirit was poured out on the Day of Pentecost. From that day we have been living in the last days. The next great event is the return of Jesus Christ to planet earth.

The Valley of Decision (chapter 3)

Vengeance on the nations (3:1–16a)

Where? The final chapter has a vision of the Valley of Decision. It is the Kidron Valley on the eastern side of Jerusalem, and to this day it is called the Valley of Judgement. It is full of Jewish graves because it is believed to be the place of resurrection when God will make his decision about our eternal destiny. It is also called the Valley of Decision, but I have heard that name misused by preachers. Joel says there are multitudes in the Valley of Decision, and so preachers use this to encourage unbelievers to make up their minds about God. Actually it is the valley in which God decides who goes to heaven and who goes to hell. It is the valley of his decision, when he will have the last word. It is his decision that decides our eternal destiny.

Why? God's decision will depend on how people have treated his people, his purpose and what he has done in the world. The nations of Tyre, Sidon and Philistia are especially singled out as ripe for judgement. The last word is that God will vindicate his people and restore them to their land.

How? The nations are called to come and fight, though there is a certain amount of sarcasm in the call, for who can 'fight' against God? The nations are told to beat their plough-shares into swords and their pruning-hooks into spears (note the very opposite in Isaiah 2:4 and Micah 4:3). Zephaniah speaks of the meeting of the nations in his prophecy.

Vindication of Israel (3:16b–21)

The final section focuses upon the restoration of Judah. She will be inhabited and fertile but, by contrast, Egypt will be desolate and Edom will be a desert, because of the violence which they have committed against Judah.

This raises a very big question upon which there are deeply divided opinions in the Church today. Obadiah, Joel and many other prophets end their prophecies with promises for the future of Israel. Since many of these remain unfulfilled, we must ask when they will be fulfilled.

There are four different opinions in the Church today, and although mine is not that of the majority, I believe it is the one that is most faithful to Scripture.

The opinions divide upon whether the promises should be taken literally or spiritually. Are we to assume that Israel will literally recover the land that God promised, or do we see the land as being symbolic of spiritual blessings, now applied to the Church, as the new Israel. This latter view is called 'replacement theology' and is probably the view of the majority of preachers in the UK.

My problem with this view is that, while they claim all the old blessings for the Church, they don't apply the curses also – these stay with Israel! God told Israel that she would be blessed if she was obedient and cursed if she was not.

The blessings included life, health, prosperity, fertility, respect and safety. The curses were disease, drought, death, danger, destruction, defeat, deportation, destitution and disgrace.

With replacement theology, the old Israel has lost the land because she was not obedient. But the blessings are applied to the Church, the new Israel, without any mention of the curses if the Church is not obedient.

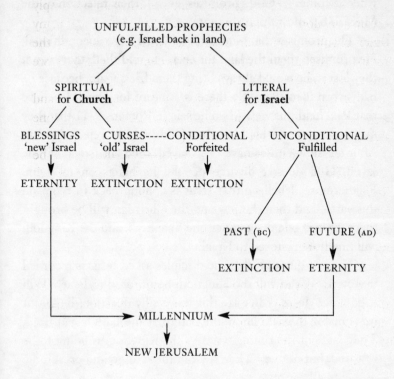

Those who believe that the promises apply to Israel literally are also divided into two groups. One group say the promises were all conditional and have been forfeited by Israel, and so there is no future for Israel as the people of God. We can evangelize Israel, but just as we would any other nation. They are now just a nation – they are no longer God's people.

But this argument does not fit in with the New Testament. Of the 74 New Testament references to 'Israel', none refer to the Church. Furthermore, there are references to the continuing throne of David, the house of Jacob and the 12 tribes of Israel. The assumption is that Israel is very much alive and well when it comes to God's promises, even if their rejection of the Messiah has meant punishment.

The promises that God made to Israel were unconditional. He promised them the land for ever. He told them that even if they lost it, he would always bring them back again, because he had sworn it to them. So there is a future for Israel. I believe that Paul held this view when he said in Romans 9–11 that they may have rejected his God, but God had not rejected them. After all the Gentiles have been saved, then 'all Israel' will be saved. God doesn't divorce people; he hangs on to them. Furthermore, I believe that Jesus is coming back to reign on this earth, and then the Jew and the Christian will be brought together into one flock under one Shepherd, and the Kingdom will finally be restored to Israel.

The last question that the disciples asked Jesus is recorded in Acts 1: 'When will the Kingdom be restored to Israel? Will it be now?' Jesus didn't say this was a silly question; he said it was not for them to know the date that the Father had fixed. They just got the timing wrong. The Kingdom is going to be restored, but not yet. Then he told them to go and preach the gospel to all nations.

So you have to face the fact that there are all these different views and all of them finish up with the old Israel becoming extinct – apart from the one I accept. I believe that the promises of God can't be broken. Indeed, if God can't hang on to Israel, he can't hang on to us either.

Conclusion

The prophecy of Joel teaches us important things about the character of God and the nature of his activity with his people and in the world around us. Joel's prophecies have been partially fulfilled, but we await their final fulfilment, when God will wind up this phase of history and bring his people to himself, as he promised.

PART III

AMOS AND HOSEA

Introduction

Amos and Hosea prophesied during the eighth century BC and the two books named after them are among the earliest included in the Bible. Although their focus was upon the northern kingdom (i.e. Israel rather than Judah), it is useful to set their preaching within the context of what was happening elsewhere in the world, especially since aspects of modern society can be traced back to this era. We will then look at the situation in Israel before examining the work of the prophets separately.

What man was doing

History records that Rome and Carthage were founded in the eighth century BC. Great rivalry between the two cities led to the Punic Wars, in which Rome was finally triumphant. From this victory came the foundations of the Roman empire. Roman law was gradually established, soon followed by the vast road-building projects which were to characterize the Romans' reign and would enable the gospel to spread some 700 years later.

Also during this century, the Olympic Games began in Greece – man's obsession with sport has ancient roots! But more significant was the spread of the Greek language throughout the Mediterranean, with Homer being one of the best-known Greek writers. The Greeks established many city-states and developed a new form of government known as democracy (though their approach was some way short of the emancipation that we associate with the word today).

In the East the Chinese and Indian civilizations were also emerging, so that there is a sense in which Israel and Judah were located at the centre of the growth of civilization, with developing cultures to the east and to the west and many travellers passing through the land.

What God was doing

God's relationship with his people had reached a difficult phase. His intention was that they should be a model to the world of what a relationship with him was like. This was why he had placed them at the 'crossroads' of the world. His covenant with them, made at Sinai in the time of Moses, stated that if they obeyed him he would bless them more than any other people, and if they disobeyed him they would be cursed more than any other people. So they were faced with a privilege and a responsibility. But by the eighth century God was faced with the dilemma of what to do with a people who were far from him.

Two kingdoms

A brief outline of their recent history will help to explain God's concerns. By the eighth century BC the people of God had been split into two. They had become a kingdom with a visible king, as they had wanted some 200 years before, but they had to endure all that went with kingship – taxation to finance the king's lavish lifestyle and conscription to defend the land.

But this kingdom had just three kings before it split. The first, Saul, was the 'people's choice' – good-looking, handsome and tall, but with some serious weaknesses of character.

When he failed to live in obedience to God's word, God gave the people a man of his own choosing – David – who is described in 1 Samuel as 'a man after God's own heart'. Despite an excellent start, he too was led into sin. One lustful look led him to break five of the Ten Commandments and he was never the same afterwards. The decline in Israel's power began on that afternoon.

The third king was Solomon, David's son. He brought great glory to the kingdom – during his reign Israel's empire was at its height – but he did so by heavy taxation and forced labour. He left the legacy of a magnificent Temple but a divided people. The northern tribes were unhappy about the fact that the kingdom's resources had been concentrated on Jerusalem in the south.

Civil war ensued as soon as Solomon died. The north rebelled against the south, and eventually the kingdom was divided, with the ten tribes in the north taking the name Israel and the two tribes in the south, who stayed loyal to Jerusalem and to the royal line, taking the name Judah.

This meant, of course, that the north was without a temple and without a royal line. They established their own holy shrines at Bethel and Samaria and their own royal line, independent of the bloodline of David that God had promised to bless.

The history of Israel in 1 and 2 Kings tells the desperate story of the reigns of these northern kings. The average length of their reigns was three years. Many of them were assassinated, and there were a number of coups. It was an unstable government, but this is not surprising, for this was not a government based on God's chosen royal line.

The south fared better, its kings reigning for an average of 33 years. (Interestingly, Jesus is believed to have been this age when he died.)

Social conditions

Peace

It is important that we understand the social conditions of the north as we seek to understand the messages that Amos and Hosea spoke. It was an era of peace and prosperity. Assyria was the superpower of the day, but Jonah's visit to Nineveh had effectively postponed their threat to Israel for some time. That generation of Assyrians had repented of their evil warmongering, and so the fear of Assyrian invasion was over, for the time being.

Prosperity

As a result, Israel now enjoyed a time of great prosperity, especially under King Jeroboam II, whose rule for a time stabilized the nation. Its economy benefited from being on the trade routes between Europe and Arabia, and a number of merchants and bankers became very wealthy.

'Haves' and 'have nots'

Although the standard of living rose, society became divided between the 'haves' and the 'have nots'. Many enjoyed the consumer society with its luxury goods. The height of fashion was to have a second home – what they called a 'summerhouse' – to which you would go in the heat of the summer, usually up in the hills. A new aristocracy developed – the 'get rich quick' boys. But housing became a problem, because as the rich got richer the poor got poorer. The rich had second homes but many people didn't even have one at all.

Moral effects

Morally the effects of all this affluence were very clear. There were financial scandals, bribery and corruption, with even the judiciary being corrupted. There was no justice in the courts without bribing the judges. They were soon into seven-days-a-week trading because they could make more money that way. Avarice led to injustice and affluence led to permissiveness. Sexual laxity was the order of the day and alcohol consumption rose sharply. Although this was 2,700 years ago, the parallels with our modern Western culture are all too easy to see.

Religious life

Religious life was also booming, but it was not the religion of Israel. Rather, the people had become interested in the faiths of the other nations, and in particular they had turned to those of the indigenous peoples of Canaan. This included the faiths of the East and the West that arrived with the travelling merchants and the Canaanite peoples' cult of 'mother nature'. Indeed, at the temples at Bethel and Samaria the worshippers had sex with male and female prostitutes, believing that this would persuade God to bless their crops. They even set up a golden calf at Bethel in a direct contradiction of God's laws against graven images. So God's holy people, who were supposed to be a royal priesthood and a holy nation, had become just like everybody else.

God would have been justified in washing his hands of them and trying to start again with another people. But God is not like that. He was married to the people of Israel, and he hates divorce. Having made a covenant with them, he was determined to stay with it. However, he couldn't turn a blind eye to their behaviour. In the giving of the Law at the time of Moses he promised that he would be forced to curse them if they were disobedient, and the Books of Amos and Hosea relate the ways in which he brought discipline to his people.

God's discipline

A food shortage

Since the people were embracing fertility cults, it was appropriate that God should demonstrate that their sexual promiscuity did not have a positive effect on the harvest. Instead a number of harvests failed. God was saying, 'Wake up! You're dependent on me, not on the fertility goddesses'. But after this disaster, as with the others, came the refrain, 'Yet you did not return to me.' In spite of the food shortage, they carried on with their pagan rituals.

A water shortage

Next, God sent a shortage of fresh drinking water, which was, of course, a great calamity in a land that was dependent upon regular rain.

Diseased and ravaged crops

An attack of mildew and locusts destroyed the crops, which led to food shortages for the animals. It may seem obvious that a people who were in covenant relationship with God should turn to him to ask what had gone wrong, but Israel refused to do so.

Plagues and raids

The crops and animals had already suffered. Now God sent plagues upon the people, and enemy raids took away their livestock. We can see that each discipline was more severe than the last. Now people were being directly affected. But still they didn't return to God.

Storms bring fire

God also allowed lightning to strike some of their cities, resulting in the destruction of vast areas of housing. But none of this had any effect. As long as they could keep their money and enjoy their holiday homes, they didn't care.

On top of God's warnings came two further disasters. It was as if God was desperate to get their attention.

An earthquake

This was much more than a little earth tremor. Some 250 years later it is mentioned in Zechariah as *the* earthquake. It demonstrated God's power over the natural realm and reminded the people of the fragility of human life. Yet still the people refused to return to God.

Exile

Eventually God's final sanction was for them to be invaded and deported by the Assyrians, never to return again. This happened in 721 BC, 30 years after Amos and 10 years after Hosea. This may seem a heavy price to pay for disobedience, but God had warned Israel about it time and again, not just through the discipline and the disasters but also through the ministries of these two prophets, who underlined and explained what God was doing and what he might be forced to do.

Indeed, Amos 3:7 says, 'Surely the Sovereign Lord does nothing without revealing his plan to his servants the prophets.' God is so amazingly merciful that he never punishes without sending a prophet first to explain to the people what will happen if they continue in their behaviour. In the New Testament the Book of Revelation is a warning of what God is going to do with the whole world, but still people don't turn to him. How much more can God do?

The 'last chance' prophets

So Amos and Hosea were the 'last chance' prophets sent to Israel, warning them of what God would be forced to do if they failed to turn back to him. The two prophets were very different. Amos was tough; Hosea was tender. Amos came with strong accusations of what they were doing wrong; Hosea came with a strong appeal to return to the Lord. If Amos spoke to their minds, Hosea spoke to their hearts. Amos majored on the justice of God, Hosea on God's mercy. Amos communicated God's thoughts to the nation, but Hosea communicated God's feelings. There is some overlap between the two prophets, but these broad characteristics shine through their messages. It is interesting that God's very last words in Hosea are a very tender, emotional appeal, hoping that Israel would repent and allow him to refrain from the judgement that he would have to execute.

AMOS	HOSEA
Rural southerner	Urban northerner
Warning	Wooing
Tough Accusation	Tender appeal
Justice of God	Mercy of God
Divine wrath	Divine love
His purity	His pity
Social sin	Spiritual sin
Injustice	Idolatry
International	National
'Seek God'	'Know God'

The Book of Amos

In the year 750 BC a man appeared in Bethel, stood on the temple steps and preached. His accent betrayed him as a southerner, so he was guaranteed to receive a hostile reaction because of who he was and what he was saying.

By profession, Amos was the poorest kind of farmer. He was a herdsman and also looked after sycamore trees, which was regarded as the very lowest job because sycamore figs tended to be the food of the poor. So he had no religious training and was not an obvious candidate for preaching, but under God's hand and by God's grace he was exactly the right man for the job.

His home town was Tekoa, 12 miles south of Jerusalem, in the heart of the southern kingdom, on the borders of the desert. God spoke to this man from the bottom rung of the social ladder, saying, 'You're the man to go and tell the northerners what is going to come to them.'

Chapter 7 of the Book of Amos gives us a remarkable insight into his personal life and his reaction to what he encountered. This chapter shows us two remarkable things:

1 His praying affected God;
2 His preaching angered men.

His praying affected God

On one occasion God showed him two pictures: the first was of locusts devouring everything in the countryside, and the second was of a fire destroying everything in the towns. He was profoundly shocked by the vision and so he said to God, 'Sovereign Lord, I beg you not to do that!' He asked God how Jacob (i.e. God's people) could survive such an onslaught. He pleaded with God not to do it, and so God drew back from what he had said he would do.

Two things are remarkable about the conversation. The first is that prayer can affect God in that way. God seems to change his course of action according to the pleading of Amos. Moses had the same experience and, of course, Jesus on the cross prayed, 'Father, forgive them. They don't know what they're doing.' The lesson of the conversation between Amos and God is clear. Our praying will never change his character but it can change his plans. This is not an impersonal God who sets things in stone, but a God who listens to us, a God who wants us to persuade him.

The second thing is that Amos speaks of the nation as 'Jacob' rather than 'Israel'. In so doing he refers to the corrupt

schemer, the man who deceived his own father to get a blessing, who was renamed Israel. It is as if Amos is deliberately
reminding God of the inconspicuous past of the man who gave
the nation its name. It is a perfect way of saying in one word
that Israel had gone back to being what Jacob had been before
he met God and wrestled with the angel.

Also in chapter 7 Amos has a vision of the Lord standing
alongside a wall with a plumb line in his hand. God was showing Amos that he was measuring Israel against his standards,
not their own, and that judgement must follow.

His preaching angered men

Predictably, the preaching of Amos angered the religious leaders. Prophets are not popular with priests or pastors. Prophets
are typically against the status quo and hence are a threat.
Amaziah the priest is especially concerned about the effect that
Amos was having and ended up opposing him. But, undaunted,
Amos preached on, predicting the demise of Jereboam, his wife
and his family.

God gave Amos his messages in two ways. He had visions
while he was awake and dreams while he was asleep. An Old
Testament prophet was known as a 'seer' because he saw things
that other people didn't see. He could see what was really
going on; he could see into the future.

The biblical text frequently tells us about what Amos saw.
One of the most telling pictures, forming a climax to his
prophecy, is a basket of fruit that is so ripe that it is on the
verge of going bad. The message was clear: Israel was ripe for
rottenness.

He also pictured God himself, invariably as a lion. In those
days there were still lions in the land of Israel. They lived in

the jungle along the Jordan River and came up into the hills looking for lambs, so lions were familiar to the people.

Amos says, 'God the lion has roared. Who will not tremble?' He gives a graphic picture of what will happen to Israel. He says it will be like a lamb caught by a lion. The shepherd may rescue an ear and a couple of legs from the lion's mouth. This is all that will be left of Israel – an ear and a couple of legs. It is vivid picture language that catches people's interest and imagination. God was known as the shepherd of Israel, so it must have been a shock for them to hear him being depicted as a lion.

Themes in Amos

The prophecy of Amos is a collection of sermons, with no clear structure. For this reason it is difficult to analyse the book as a whole. It is as if the book plants time bombs in people's hearts, ready to go off at an appropriate time in the future.

A number of themes can be identified:

Eight sentences (chapters 1:1–2:16)

1 Damascus
2 Gaza
3 Tyre
4 Edom
5 Ammon
6 Moab
7 Judah
8 Israel

Three sermons (chapters 3–6)

1 'Yet you have not returned'
2 'Seek me and live'
3 'Woe …'

Five symbols (chapters 7–8)

1 A plague of locusts
2 Fire devours the deep
3 A plumb line
4 A basket of ripe fruit
5 The destruction of the ripe fruit

Three surprises (chapter 9)

1 The rebuilding of David's house
2 The return of the people
3 The fertility of the land

A poetic book

Although there is little structure, the choice of genre is quite deliberate. Throughout the Bible a distinction can be made between poetry and prose. The former gives us God's feelings about a situation, the latter God's thoughts. Many are unaware that the Bible is full of God's emotions. God is full of feelings. We need to understand what makes him angry, what makes him sad, what makes him feel sick, what makes him happy. People become obsessed with their feelings about God, but actually our future depends on his feelings about us.

Some poetry is very light and lifts you, but some is very heavy, and is called a dirge. The poetry in Amos falls into the latter category.

Repetition

Amos also uses repetition, which is especially effective when speaking. He wants his hearers to remember the message that although God has sent troubles, they have not returned to him. So he repeats the refrain: 'You did not return to me.'

But let's look at chapter 1 and see how skilfully he structures his words. His refrain in this section is 'For three sins, even for four'.

The inhumanity of Israel's neighbours

He starts by condemning Israel's neighbours. He focuses on Damascus and how they deserve God's punishment. Damascus was not part of the people of God, so it was dealt with for inhumanity and cruelty in particular. Then he rails on Gaza, which was noted for its brutality, then on Tyre for its treachery. No doubt Amos' audience agreed with the message so far.

The infamy of Israel's cousins

Then he moves on to the ethnic cousins of Israel – Edom, Ammon and Moab. He says God will deal with Edom for their ruthlessness, with Ammon for their barbarity, and with Moab for treating sacred things profanely. His audience are still with him at this point in his talk.

The infidelity of Israel's sister

Next he moves a little closer to home, condemning Israel's sister Judah. God will deal with Judah for rejecting the laws of God and accepting the lies of men.

The insensitivity of Israel's children

Then comes the shock. Just when he has the audience with him, he tells them that God will deal with them too. He tells them that they have become so used to sin that they have forgotten how to blush. What is worse, they don't seem to realize it. The main message for Israel is that past redemption means future retribution. Since God chose them out of all the families of the earth, he must punish them more severely. The terms of the Sinai covenant were divine blessings on obedience and divine curses on disobedience, which the people had voluntarily, even eagerly, accepted. Israel could be blessed more than other nations – or cursed more. It is a divine principle that of those who are given much, much is expected. Extra privileges bring greater responsibility.

This is a principle that runs through even to the New Testament. Christians are among those who have heard the gospel, who know the commandments, and therefore God will deal with them more severely.

Another sermon that uses repetition is full of the word 'woe'. It is a series of curses upon those who have been disobedient. Amos tells them that many of those who long for the Day of the Lord are mistaken about what that Day will mean. They are presuming that all will be well. They are complacent in their decadent lifestyles. But they must realize that ritual is no substitute for righteousness and sacrifice is no substitute for sanctification.

The theme 'Seek me and live' is the basis for another sermon. They are told to stop seeking comfort in the land and instead to seek the Lord. They are to seek righteousness. If they do, the Lord will hear them and forgive.

Amos' final message

The last message sounds especially fierce. The vision of the fruit suggests that Israel is 'ripe for judgement'. God says he will never forget them – he records everything. He only forgets what he has forgiven, but the rest he never forgets. Amos tells them that the 10 tribes of Israel will be scattered among the nations, never to rise again. But in the midst of this terrible permanent sentence, it's as if the sun breaks through the clouds, for God says, 'But not all of you. Only the sinners in Israel will disappear. There will be a remnant. I will build again the tabernacle of David and bring Gentiles in to take your place in the people of God.' So a remnant that will keep true to God will survive and will be part of an enlarged people of God that will include Gentiles.

Indeed, these words of prophecy were quoted 800 years later in Acts 15, when the Council of Jerusalem met to consider the grounds for the admission of Gentiles into the Church. The leader of the church in Jerusalem reminded the council of the prophecy of Amos, in which God had promised that he would restore the tabernacle of David and bring the Gentiles in.

The Book of Hosea

Ten years after Amos had preached in Bethel, another prophet came on the scene. He was to be God's last prophet to the northern 10 tribes of Israel. We have already noted that Hosea's ministry was a real contrast to that of Amos. This time it's affection rather than accusation, wooing rather than warning, tender rather than tough, mercy rather than justice. It is God's final appeal before the 10 tribes disappear.

A key word unlocks the whole prophecy. It is the Hebrew word *chesed* (the *ch* is pronounced like the 'ch' in 'loch'). The word has no exact English equivalent. It is essentially a covenant word, used to describe those with whom you have a covenant relationship. It does mean 'love', but it has an awful lot of the word 'loyalty' in it too. True love is not true love unless it is loyal.

Chesed is often translated as 'loving kindness' or 'faithful-ness'. 'Faithfulness' is used 60 times for this word in our English Bibles, while 'kindness' is used 9 or 10 times. It means unswerv-ing love and undying devotion – it means we're so committed to someone that we go on loving them, whatever happens.

The old English word 'troth' is close (the word 'betrothed' is still used by some). It may be very significant that the word 'troth' itself has died out, because this kind of loyalty has died out too. Love is too often known without loyalty. People enjoy love with someone for a while, then drop them for someone else.

A covenant love

The whole relationship between God and Israel is a covenant love and therefore a *chesed*, stay-with-it love. Indeed, the Book of Hosea depicts the covenant love of God for his bride, Israel.

On God's side

God covenanted to look after them, protect them and provide for them. He had rescued them from Egypt and at Sinai had offered them the opportunity to be his people, which they had accepted. He was looking for glad, eager obedience – for a bride who wanted to live the way he wanted her to live.

On Israel's side

Israel was to respond joyfully to God's demands, knowing that because they were given for their good, they would be a delight to obey. David's Psalms express his delight in the Law of God. The longest Psalm in the Bible (119) is entirely about the ben-efits of the Law. But as a whole, the people of God did not obey and, by the time of Hosea, their failure was most pronounced.

God had to say through Hosea's messages, 'What's happened to our marriage?' He assured them of his loyal love but was certain that he was receiving very little back.

In order for Hosea to understand God's feelings, God took him through an extraordinary experience. God often prepared a prophet through his relationships or lack of them. God told Jeremiah that he must not marry, because he had to tell Judah that God too was now a bachelor. From the loneliness of not having a wife Jeremiah learned how God was feeling without Israel. Ezekiel was told that his wife would die but he must not weep for her, in order to show Judah that God too had been bereaved of his wife. In the same way, Hosea was taught how God felt by obeying some unusual instructions with regard to his marriage situation.

The background (chapters 1–3)

Chapters 1–3 give the background to the story. They are autobiographical and, indeed, are so fantastic that scholars argue whether it's fact or fiction, or whether the order of the chapters is different from the order of the events. But I believe we are safe to take it in its plainest, simplest meaning.

The first three chapters give us the storyline of the prophecy.

Chapter 1: the children

Hosea was told to marry a prostitute – something as shocking then as it would be today, especially for someone whom God intended to be his spokesman. They had three children, at least one of whom was not Hosea's. Then his wife returned to her old occupation. Hosea found her, brought her home and put her through a period of discipline when he didn't know her as a wife. He then courted her and started all over again with her as his wife.

The names of the children carry their own message. The first was a boy called Jezreel, which means 'God sows it'. He was a very rebellious, unruly child who had to be disciplined.

The second child was a girl called Lo-Ruhamah, which means 'not pitied'. This was a deprived child who didn't have love from her mother.

The third child was a boy called Lo-Ammi, which means 'not my people'. He was the child whom Hosea didn't father, and so the boy was disowned. So we have: disciplined, deprived and disowned. The children summarize how God was dealing with his people Israel. The names of the children were important to the message, though I haven't met any Christian parents who have used any of those three names!

Chapter 2: the wife

Chapter 2 tells us three things about Hosea's wife. First, she was reproached by her own children for what she was doing. They knew she was doing wrong. Secondly, Hosea punished her for her behaviour, and finally she was restored as his wife. The alliteration once again is clear: reproached, requited, restored.

Chapter 3: the husband

The pattern of threes continues with Hosea himself. We are told three things about him in chapter 3.

First, he was faithful to his wife even when she was faithless to him.

Secondly, he was firm with her, and for a period he did not treat her as his wife. He brought her home but didn't share the bed with her – representing the period of discipline in the exile that God was going to put the Jews through.

Thirdly, he was feared. His wife had a healthy fear of him, and trembled when she was with him. It meant that respect and loyalty were slowly being brought back into her life.

The message (chapters 4–14)

Chapters 4–14 give us the message that grew out of this relationship. Like the Book of Amos, Hosea is a collection of the
prophet's sermons, presented in no particular order. Nevertheless, we can put it together under various headings, which
give us the main themes and enable us to read it with understanding.

We must realize that everything Hosea says centres around
these two headings: *Israel's unfaithfulness* and *God's faithfulness*.
It is the contrast between the *chesed* that comes from God and
the lack of response from the people that forms the theme of
his whole prophecy.

This sums up God's argument with Israel, and his compassion for them comes out of this dilemma: What do you do with
a people whom you love but who are unfaithful to you?

Israel's unfaithfulness

Hosea identifies seven sins, which we will call the 'seven deadly
sins of Israel'. Their record shows God's detailed knowledge of
what was going on.

1 **Infidelity** The people had become unfaithful in their marriages as well as unfaithful to God.
2 **Independence** God's chosen government was in
   Jerusalem, but they had created their own royal line with
   their own independent kingdom. And independence is, of
   course, the essence of sin. They effectively said they would
   not have God to rule over them. They preferred their own
   kingdom and were in active rebellion against God's chosen
   king in the south.
3 **Intrigue** The lack of loyalty towards God was mirrored in
   the people's disloyalty towards each other. This was seen in

people talking behind each other's backs, secret agreements being concocted and many people being upset.

4 **Idolatry** The golden calf of Samaria figures large in Hosea's prophecy. The people were openly accepting the Canaanite gods and engaging in pagan worship. The high places of Canaanite religion were being revered.

5 **Immorality** The bull was a symbol of fertility, and sexual immorality became common. The laws regarding sexual practices in the books of Moses had been jettisoned in favour of the lax morality of the surrounding nations. We have noted already that such immorality was even regarded as 'religious', in spite of its opposition to God's holy Law.

6 **Ignorance** The response to Hosea's prophecy made it clear that Israel was largely ignorant of the ways in which God's holy Law was being ignored. But it wasn't just that they didn't know about God – they didn't *want* to know about God.

7 **Ingratitude** God underlines the ingratitude of their behaviour by giving Hosea a series of pictures which would stick in their minds.

In chapter 7 Hosea uses a variety of images to describe the character of Israel, and none are complimentary. He said their evil passions were like a heated oven ready to bake the dough. He also compared them to an unturned cake that's getting all burnt on one side but uncooked on the other. Such a cake is completely inedible – a picture of the compromise of the nation. Its half-heartedness makes it effectively useless.

Hosea continues with the image of the fluttering dove trapped in a net. Israel has kept faith with no one, least of all God. She turns to Egypt one moment and Assyria the next – but never to God. So he must capture and discipline her.

The guilty parties

Hosea follows his list of deadly sins by identifying four groups of people whom he believes are responsible for this condition.

1 **The priests** They should have known God and should have been reminding the people of the Law of God so that if they sinned, sacrifice was available. But they had abrogated their responsibility. Those who should have been an example were just as bad as the rest.

2 **The prophets** Israel was not without a large number of prophets. But they were all false prophets. They would tell the people of God not to worry about their behaviour, claiming that God wouldn't do the dreadful things he had promised – which, of course, was exactly what they wanted to hear. But God needs men who will tell the people what they don't want to hear, even when it's costly.

3 **The princes (or kings)** Although God had not chosen the northern royal line, they were still responsible for the people. In some respects the kings were like pastors to the people, responsible for ensuring that they were obedient to God's Law. However, few of the kings were at all concerned with how the nation had responded. Many of the people would take their lead from the kings. When they saw immorality at the head of the nation, they assumed it was OK for them to do likewise.

4 **The profiteers** Many were making big money out of the housing market, and the poor lost out every time. The Law of God was clear on the evils of charging interest and exploiting the poor. Hosea singles out the profiteers as the corrupters of society.

The punishments

Hosea tells them that suffering is coming in three areas.

1 **Barrenness** He says there will be miscarriages, and some
   women will not even be able to conceive. Others will lose
   their babies when they are born.
2 **Bloodshed** Next God predicts that an enemy will attack
   and kill many of them. He will not defend them.
3 **Banishment** Ultimately this enemy will be victorious and
   will evict them from the land.

God's faithfulness

These punishments are the severe side of Hosea's prophecy.
Although he is more tender than Amos, he is not without a
hard-hitting challenge. But it's not his main thrust. The major
theme is that, in spite of their widespread disobedience, God is
still faithful.

There's a statement in 1 Timothy about our relationship to
Jesus. It says that if we deny him or if we disown him, he will
disown us, but if we are faithless to him, then he remains faithful. That might have been lifted straight out of Hosea.

For the good news is that God has compassion on the people of Israel. This is the real heart of Hosea's word.

We can use the letters ' G-O-D' as an aid to memory
(though not in the right order).

Because of his love for them God cannot let them *Off*, he
cannot let them *Go* and he cannot let them *Down*.

GOD CAN'T LET THEM OFF (5:10–6:6)

This passage depicts God's hatred of their professions of
repentance. He says, 'I will tear Ephraim and Judah as a lion
rips apart its prey. I will carry them off and chase all rescuers
away. I will abandon them and return to my home until they

admit their guilt and look to me for help again.' He says that as soon as trouble comes they typically talk about returning to the Lord who will help them, without any real intention of changing their hearts. So God has to say, 'What shall I do with you? For your love vanishes like morning clouds. It disappears like dew. I sent my prophets to warn you of your doom. I have slain you with the words in my mouth, threatening you with death. I don't want your sacrifices – I want your love. I don't want your offerings – I want you to know me.'

GOD CAN'T LET THEM GO (11:1–11)

God makes his appeal to them, reminding them of the time when Israel was a child. God loved him as a son and brought him up out of Egypt. But the more God called to him, the more he rebelled, sacrificing to Baal and burning incense to idols. Although God had trained him from infancy, taught him how to walk and held him in his arms, Israel treated God with considerable scorn.

But God cries, 'How can I give you up, my Ephraim? How can I let you go? My heart cries out within me! How I long to help you! No, I will not punish you as much as my fierce anger tells me to. For I am God and not man, I am the Holy One living among you, and I didn't come to destroy.'

We see here a powerful expression of God's feelings. Whatever happens, he knows he cannot let them go.

GOD CAN'T LET THEM DOWN (14:1–9)

This passage is an impassioned appeal by God for the people to return to him and allow him to cure them of their idolatrous behaviour. It is not that Israel has mistakenly sinned – she has been defiant in her pursuit of evil. But God tells them that if they repent, he will forgive them. He will never let them down.

The passage finishes with a statement: 'Whoever is wise, let him understand these things, and whoever is intelligent, let him listen. For the paths of the Lord are true and right, and good men walk along them, but sinners trying it will fail.' It is one of the strongest appeals in the whole of the Bible to people who don't want to know about God's love, and it finishes the prophecy. Israel is given a final choice – to follow the ways of the Lord or to continue in waywardness.

How do we apply Amos and Hosea today?

First, we must concede that neither Amos nor Hosea succeeded in bringing Israel back to God. Their messages went unheeded, and God was forced to judge the people in the way he had promised. In 721 BC, Assyria defeated them and took them into exile, never to return.

Next, we must note that there is a big difference between our situation and that to which Amos and Hosea spoke and prophesied. In Israel there was a theocratic government; the Church and the State were one and the same thing. But this does not apply in the New Testament, where Church and State are clearly separated. The New Testament situation is summed up by Jesus' words, 'Render to Caesar the things that are Caesar's and to God the things that are God's.' So Christians today live in two kingdoms. I am a citizen of the United Kingdom, according to my passport. I am also a citizen of the Kingdom of God. So we have to be careful when applying Old Testament prophecies to our modern situation.

We suffer from a complication brought about by the Emperor Constantine in the fourth century AD. Europe has tried to combine Church and State. Constantine tried to create a Christendom in which the Kingdom of God and the kingdoms of man are one and the same thing, and the legacy remains in many European nations. So to be born into England is to be born into the Church, and we have centuries of an established Christianity behind us. But as far as God is concerned, the Church and the State are separate. We can make applications from Old Testament prophecies, but we must bear in mind that the two situations are not directly comparable.

So we cannot take a message from Amos or Hosea and say that the nation must obey in the way that God expected Israel to obey. But where the prophecy is directed to the people outside Israel, a legitimate application can be made. God's accusations to the other nations were based on conscience, not on the Law of God. In the same way, a secular nation will be judged on the basis of whether they lived according to what they intrinsically knew to be right.

So some of the sins that Amos and Hosea condemn in non-Israelite nations do apply. This includes inhumanity, riding roughshod over human rights, and legislation that makes the rich richer and the poor poorer. These are areas that we can apply validly.

However, this is not to say that the rest of prophecies to Israel are irrelevant. They do carry a powerful message to the Church today. For the Church too often behaves in a fashion similar to that of the people of Israel. There are plenty of New Testament passages that reinforce the messages of Hosea and Amos. We too must return to God, lest we come under his judgement. So when we read these prophecies, we must apply them to the people of God first, and then we are in a position to tell society what God says to them about the way they are living.

PART IV

ISAIAH

Introduction

Isaiah is a fascinating book to study. For a start, the documents of the prophecy of Isaiah are among the best attested of all the books in the Old Testament. The Dead Sea Scrolls, found in 1948, included a copy of the book that dated from 100 BC, which was around a thousand years older than the next oldest copy, which dated from 900 AD. At the time translation work on the Revised Standard Version of the Bible was being completed, but the work was stopped while these documents were checked. But very little needed changing.

Isaiah is also fascinating because of the way the book has been arranged in our Bibles. The chapter headings in the Bible are not inspired. (I wish we had a Bible without chapter and verse numbers, because then we would know our Bibles according to the flow of thought, and not in an artificial way according to 'texts', as we do today. For at least 1,100 years the Christian Church had Bibles without any chapter and verse numbers.)

But whoever divided Isaiah into chapters did a rather interesting thing, though I doubt whether it was deliberate. They divided the book into 66 chapters, the same number as the books of the Bible. Furthermore, they divided Isaiah into two distinct parts of 39 chapters and 27 chapters. It just happens that the Old Testament has 39 books and the New Testament 27.

Also, the message of the first 39 chapters summarizes the message of the Old Testament, and the message of the last 27 chapters summarizes exactly the message of the New Testament! The second part of Isaiah (i.e. chapter 40) begins with the voice crying in the wilderness, 'Prepare the way for the Lord' – words later used by John the Baptist. It moves on to a servant of the Lord who is anointed by the Holy Spirit, dies for the sins of his people, and is raised and exalted after his death. It then moves on to the declaration that 'You shall be my witnesses to the ends of the earth', and it finishes up with God saying, 'I am making all things new. I create a new heaven and a new earth.'

In other words, if somebody took the whole Bible and squeezed it into one book, you'd finish up with the prophecy of Isaiah. It is the Bible in miniature.

Even more remarkable is the fact that chapters 40–66 divide very clearly into three sections, each of nine chapters. So in chapters 40–48 the theme is comforting God's people; in chapters 49–57 the theme is the Servant of the Lord, who dies and rises again; and chapters 58–66 are about the future glory.

Furthermore, each of these sections of nine chapters divides into three sections of three chapters. If you take the middle three there are three very clear sections; 49–51, 52–54 and 55–57. If you take the middle section (chapters 52–54), and the middle verse of the middle chapter of that middle section, you come to the key verse in the book: 'He was pierced for our transgressions, he was crushed for our iniquities; the punishment that brought us peace was upon him, and by his wounds we are healed' (53:5). None of this is inspired as such, but it is remarkable that even the central verse of the second section should sum up the central theme of the New Testament.

The Book of Isaiah is very well known in parts. I remember someone's comment after reading one of Shakespeare's plays.

He said he didn't like it because it was too full of quotations and he was sure that Shakespeare had taken a lot of his material from somewhere else, not realizing that it was Shakespeare who had originated those quotations! The same is true of the Book of Isaiah. There are many texts from it that are well known to those who have been brought up in church circles.

For example:

> Though your sins be as scarlet, they shall be as white as snow.
>
> **(1:18, AV)**

If wool has been dyed it is impossible to make it white again, but this is what God says about our sins.

> They shall beat their swords into plowshares, and their spears into pruninghooks. **(2:4, AV)**

This verse is on a block of granite outside the United Nations headquarters in New York. It is a pity that they didn't quote the whole verse, for it starts, 'He shall judge among the nations ...' Without God to judge between the nations, there is no way that anyone will ever manage to complete the second half of the verse.

Other well-known quotes include:

> A virgin shall conceive, and bear a son, and shall call his name Immanuel. **(7:14, AV)**

> For unto us a child is born, unto us a son is given: and the government shall be upon his shoulder: and his name shall be called Wonderful, Counseller, The mighty God, The everlasting Father, The Prince of Peace. **(9:6, AV)**

The spirit of the LORD shall rest upon him, the spirit of wisdom and understanding, the spirit of counsel and might, the spirit of knowledge and of the fear of the LORD.   **(11:2, AV)**

Thou wilt keep him in perfect peace, whose mind is stayed on thee.   **(26:3, AV)**

They that wait upon the LORD shall renew their strength; they shall mount up with wings as eagles; they shall run, and not be weary; and they shall walk, and not faint.   **(40:31, AV)**

How beautiful upon the mountains are the feet of him that bringeth good tidings.   **(52:7, AV)**

The Lord's hand is not shortened, that it cannot save; neither his ear heavy, that it cannot hear.   **(59:1, AV)**

Oh that thou wouldest rend the heavens, that thou wouldest come down.   **(64:1, AV)**

Another well-known section is the call of Isaiah in chapter 6, when he has a vision of God in the Temple, though his difficult mission, described in the next verses of the same chapter, is less well known. Chapter 35 describes the desert blossoming as a rose. Chapter 40 starts with the familiar words, 'Comfort ye, comfort ye my people, saith your God.' We have already mentioned 53:5, 'he was wounded for our transgressions, he was bruised for our iniquities'. Most Christians recognize 55:1, 'Come ye, buy, and eat; yea, come, buy wine and milk without money and without price.' Chapter 61 includes the text for Christ's first sermon in Nazareth: 'The Spirit of the Lord God is upon me; because the Lord hath anointed me to preach good tidings unto the meek.'

Having said that people know certain parts of the book if Isaiah, it is also clear that the book as a whole is not known at all well. This is a shame, for it is the book that both Jesus and the apostle Paul quote more than any other part of the Old Testament. The New Testament is full of quotes from it, especially from the second part.

Few Christians seem to be aware that phrases such as 'grieving the Holy Spirit', 'God shall wipe away all tears', 'a voice crying in the wilderness', 'you shall be my witnesses to the ends of the earth' and 'every knee shall bow and every tongue confess' all come straight out of the second section of Isaiah.

So it is clear that if you really want to know the Bible, you need to get to know Isaiah. It will provide you with insights into the New Testament as well as the Old.

The man

Like most biblical writers, Isaiah was a self-effacing and God-centred man, so he was loath to talk about himself. What we do know about him comes from his writings and from other Jewish historical books, in particular from the historian Josephus, who says quite a lot about Isaiah. So it is possible to piece together a picture. He must have had godly parents, for his Hebrew name, *Yesa-Yahu* ('Isaiah' is the anglicized form of this), means 'God saves'. This has a similar root to the names Jesus and Joshua. It was an entirely appropriate name, because he has been called the evangelist of the Old Testament. He is the one who brings the gospel, the good news, especially in the second part of the book. The word 'new' rarely occurs in the Old Testament, but it does occur frequently in this second part of the Book of Isaiah. He grew up to be the greatest prophet of all time, classed by the Jews in the same category as Moses and Elijah.

From a human point of view he had a head start, having been born in a palace and brought up in court. He was the grandson of King Joash and was therefore a cousin of King Uzziah, which is one reason why he was so devastated by Uzziah's death. Isaiah had wealth, rank and education. This gave him some advantages, but it also made it hard to be a prophet. But he had such an encounter with the Lord in the Temple that the path he should follow was made crystal clear.

He moved freely in court circles and counselled kings, so many of his prophecies deal with political issues, especially the false security of making alliances with powers such as Assyria or Egypt.

As far as his own family life is concerned, his wife was a prophetess, but we do not have a single prophecy from her. It is quite likely that he checked his prophecies with her before delivering them.

He had at least two sons. One of them was named *Maher-Shalal-Hash-Baz*, which means 'haste the booty, speed the spoil' – not the sort of name that most parents would choose for their offspring! But it was a prophetic name pointing to the day when Jerusalem itself would be looted by an enemy and all the treasures would be taken. The other son was called *Shear-Jashub*, which means 'a remnant shall return'. So the two sons' names sum up the two focal messages of Isaiah. The bad news (mainly in the first half of his book) is that Jerusalem will be sacked and looted and spoiled. The good news is that a remnant shall return – Israel still has a future, even after losing everything.

There is speculation that he had a third child called Emmanuel. Certainly, there was a little boy born around that time who was the subject of prophecy. Nevertheless, I think it was another man's child, not his. The child Emmanuel – whose name meant 'God with us' – was a sign to the king. He was, in fact, a double sign, which was also fulfilled centuries later in Jesus.

His call

Isaiah's call came during a visit to the Temple. He had a vision and was overcome by the holiness of the Lord. His age is not given in the text, but he was probably in his late teens or early twenties. From this moment on, Isaiah used a name for God that was not used by anyone else – 'the Holy One of Israel'. This name occurs nearly 50 times all the way through his book and in both parts of it. As soon as he caught a sight of God's holiness, he felt unclean and wanted to leave the Temple. It is interesting that he felt that his lips were unclean. He had the remarkable experience of an angel flying with a live, red-hot coal to cauterize his lips. Some think this was an imaginary vision, but it really happened. Throughout his life Isaiah would tell people that his scarred mouth was the result of God burning his lips.

The call of Isaiah gives us an unexpected reference to the Trinity. Isaiah was asked by God, 'Whom shall I send? And who will go for us?' The plural 'us' indicates that the whole Godhead would be sending him. Then comes the shattering news that, although he is being commissioned to preach to the people, they will not listen to his preaching. God will make them hard of hearing and they will not receive the word or make any response. So God is saying to Isaiah at the start of his ministry, 'Don't think you're going to be a successful preacher. The more you preach, the harder they will get! Indeed, I'm going to use your preaching to deafen them and blind them, lest they should be converted and healed.'

It's an extraordinary statement, underlining a truth found in other parts of the Bible, that the word of God not only opens people's hearts, but can also close them. It can push people further away. After we have listened to the word of God, we are either harder against it or softer towards it. But we can't remain neutral.

The verses outlining Isaiah's experience of preaching are quoted in the New Testament more often than any other verse in Isaiah. Jesus used it of his own ministry. He said he spoke so that 'they may be ever seeing but never perceiving, and ever hearing but never understanding; otherwise they might turn and be forgiven!' (Mark 4:12). In other words, he spoke in parables to hide the truth and to harden those who weren't really interested. Paul quoted the same verse when he preached to the Jews and they wouldn't listen.

So the hardening impact of the word of God is a key theme, and it is no wonder that Isaiah asked: 'How long do I have to go on preaching and hardening them with no response?' The Lord's reply came: 'Until the land is utterly forsaken.' Isaiah had one of the toughest assignments of all the prophets. But, of course, if he hadn't gone through with it, we wouldn't have this amazing book. He didn't know that centuries ahead, this book would be an inspiration. But in his lifetime he was a failure. Nobody listened – they just got harder and harder for 40 years.

The location of Judah

Our understanding of the book is aided by appreciating that Judah was surrounded by a number of nations – smaller ones close to her borders, with the larger, super-power nations further away. In Isaiah we find that God first used the small nations to discipline his people, but when they wouldn't listen, he used the bigger ones. The small nations included the

Syrians in the north and the Ammonites, the Moabites and the Edomites to the west and the south. Then to the west were the Philistines, whom God had brought from Crete, and down in the desert were the Arabs. The bigger powers were, in the east, Assyria and then Babylon, though the latter did not reach its full power until Isaiah had died. His references to Babylon speak prophetically of the power and prominence that she will one day enjoy. In the west was Egypt.

There were a number of alliances against 'little' Judah in Isaiah's day. Perhaps the most surprising was the one between the 10 tribes of Israel (i.e. the northern kingdom) and the Syrians. This was a serious moment in the history of God's people. It was at this time that Isaiah assured the king of Judah that they would win, in spite of being just two small tribes. Isaiah said, 'Behold, a virgin will conceive and bear a son and call his name Emmanuel.' This would be a sign that God would bring victory.

Emmanuel means 'God is with us', but there are four different ways of reading the phrase 'God is with us', depending on which of the four words are stressed. The emphasis should actually be on the word 'us'. God is with 'us' – not with 'them'! In other words, it means that God is on our side. So when the boy was conceived and the name was given, the king knew that the alliance between the 10 tribes and the Syrians wouldn't win.

On another occasion the Philistines linked up with the Arabs. Once again, this was a serious threat against little Judah. But again God was on their side.

In the time of Isaiah, Assyria, with its capital Nineveh on the shores of the Tigris, was the big power to the east. Egypt was the big power in the south-west. But there was also a new power growing called Babylon (in the region known today as Iraq), which would become even more powerful in the future.

Isaiah prophesied during four reigns. He began in the year when King Uzziah died and Jotham came to the throne. Ahaz, Hezekiah and finally Manasseh were also on the throne during his ministry.

The kings of Judah

In noting how Isaiah needed to preach, it is useful to note the pattern that develops when we examine the success of the kings of Judah. The Books of Kings tell us whether the king in question was good or bad in the eyes of God. The good kings won the battles and the bad kings lost. If they were good, God was with them and no one could defeat them.

Uzziah (792–740 BC) was a case in point. He was a good king to begin with and had a long reign of 52 years. But in the last years he became a bad king – he did evil in the sight of the Lord and died of leprosy. This was his punishment for changing from a good king to a bad king.

During the early years of Isaiah the first enemy attack came from the Philistines and the Arabs in a formidable alliance. But Judah won because the king followed God's ways. But when the king became disobedient, the Assyrians defeated Judah.

Jotham (750–740) was a good king who reigned for 19 years (10 of those as regent). Whoever came to attack Judah during his time was defeated. The Ammonites and also an alliance between Israel and Syria were defeated.

Ahaz (735–715) was a bad king who was defeated by the Edomites, the Philistines and the Assyrians.

Hezekiah (715–686) was a good king who reigned for 29 years and defeated the Philistines. It was during his reign that the Assyrians besieged Jerusalem with 185,000 troops, but God sent an angel to wipe them out completely. Until a few years ago many people thought that was a legend, but a British archaeologist has found human skeletons lying at the foot of the city wall, and they are believed to be the remains of this very army.

The siege of Jerusalem was the reason for an engineering work in the city that lasts to this day. Concerned about the need for water during the siege, Hezekiah dug a tunnel to bring water from a spring outside the city. It is still possible to walk through this very tunnel.

But it wasn't all good news. Hezekiah made a big mistake towards the end of his life when he fell ill. He cried to the Lord and was given 15 more years of life, but he did not use the time well. On one occasion messengers arrived with a 'Get well' card from the son of the king of Babylon – at that time a small but growing state. Hezekiah was pleased that somebody so far away was thinking about him, so he showed the visitors around his palace so that they would tell their king what a wonderful king Hezekiah was. But when Isaiah heard what had happened, he was horrified. He told Hezekiah that one day the king of Babylon would take everything that the Babylonian visitors had been shown. It's a very dramatic little narrative right in the middle of the Book of Isaiah, and it came true just as Isaiah had said.

Manasseh (695–642) was one of the worst kings of Judah. He was involved in devil worship and even sacrificed his own son to the demonic god Molech, who was the centre of the satanic worship in Judah. Most bad kings lasted just a short time, but his reign, at 53 years, was one of the longest that Judah had known.

Manasseh hated Isaiah so much that he forbade him ever to speak. This is one reason why we have the prophecy of Isaiah written down. But finally Manasseh could stand it no more and resolved to kill the prophet. It was a particularly nasty death. According to Jewish history, Manasseh ordered a hollow tree-trunk to be brought. Isaiah was tied up, pushed into the hollow tree and sawn in half. He is mentioned in Hebrews 11 as one of the 'heroes of the faith'. The words 'some were sawn in two' refer to him.

The table below outlines the different reigns in Isaiah's time:

KING	REIGN	CHARACTER	VICTORIES	DEFEATS
UZZIAH	52 years	GOOD then BAD	{ ARABS PHILISTINES	 ASSYRIANS
JOTHAM	19 years	GOOD	AMMONITES { SYRIANS ISRAELITES	
AHAZ	20 years	BAD		EDOMITES PHILISTINES ASSYRIANS
HEZEKIAH	29 years	GOOD	PHILISTINES ASSYRIANS	
MANASSEH	53 years	BAD		ASSYRIANS

The book

The first thing that strikes the reader of the Book of Isaiah is the contrast between its two parts. Like the other prophetic books, it is a collection of different messages given at different times. It is not in chronological order; sometimes it is in topical order and sometimes it is in no order at all. So it is a bit of a mixture, but on the whole one type of prophecy predominates in the first part of the book and another type predominates in the second part.

The first 39 chapters are quite different from the last 27 – so much so that many scholars think that the second part was written by someone else, referred to as 'Deutero Isaiah' ('Deutero' means 'second'). The differences between the two parts can be summarized as below:

PART 1	PART 2
More bad news than good	More good news than bad
Human activity	Divine activity
Sin and retribution	Salvation and redemption
Justice	Mercy
Confronting	Comforting
God of Israel	Creator of the universe
National	International
God = fire	God = father
God's hand	God's arm
upraised to strike	outstretched to save
Curses (woe)	Blessings
'Strange work'	Good tidings
Jews	Gentiles
Assyria	Babylon
Before the exile	After the exile
Present	Future

Since the second half is largely focused on the post-exilic period, sceptics feel that the events are given in such detail that someone else must have written it. They say that Isaiah couldn't have predicted that Babylon would be defeated by a man called Cyrus, because it happened 100 years after Isaiah had died.

So scholars suggest that 'Proto Isaiah' wrote chapters 1–39, then 'Deutero Isaiah' wrote chapters 40–56, and 'Trito Isaiah' apparently wrote the last 10 chapters. So now we have three Isaiahs! This is taught as gospel truth in some Bible schools. The reason given is that there is such a difference in style, content and vocabulary that a different author must have been responsible for each section.

The unity of the book

It is argued that whether there were three Isaiahs or one doesn't really matter. But these scholars forget that Isaiah gave many messages over a period of many years, and with a different aim – either to confront or comfort. So he would naturally use a different style and different vocabulary. It is not necessary to saw the book in two or three.

In addition, there are a number of reasons for believing that the same writer wrote all of the Book of Isaiah.

First, the two parts have so much in common. Isaiah's description of God as the 'Holy One of Israel' occurs 50 times – 25 times in Part 1 and 25 times in Part 2. While there are some themes that are covered in one part and not the other, all the major themes straddle the two parts.

Secondly, it would be amazing if the writer of Part 2 of the book, which includes what many regard as the greatest prophetic section in the whole Bible, should be forgotten. If the names of the other biblical prophets – including the minor prophets – are known, it hardly seems likely that the name of the author of the second part of Isaiah would be lost.

Thirdly, both Jesus and Paul quote from Part 2 and accredit Isaiah as the prophet. This is enough for me. I can't believe that either Jesus or Paul would lie about the authorship of Isaiah if it were uncertain.

Lastly, the key argument concerns whether or not God knows the future. If he does, then he has no difficulty in communicating that future to Isaiah. Once we settle this central issue, many of our problems are solved.

Part 1 (chapters 1–39)

The Book of Isaiah is a collection of different prophecies made over 40 years, so it is not very ordered. But there is a broad shape to it which will help our understanding as we read it. We will give a brief overview of Part 1 before looking at some of the themes in more detail.

Chapters 1–10 are a reproof for Judah and particularly for Jerusalem. The nation was wealthy, but just as Amos preaches against the inappropriate use of wealth in the northern kingdom of Israel, so Isaiah does the same in Judah. He criticizes the women of Jerusalem for the money they spend on jewellery and clothing, while neglecting the poor and disadvantaged.

Then in chapters 13–23 there is a section about judgement on other nations. God used them to discipline his people, but they overstepped God's permission in their actions. They were malicious and cruel and did more to Israel than God had intended them to do.

In chapters 24–34 there is a mixture of good and bad news. There is judgement for the northern tribes and Judah, but the coming glory is described twice. So there is a rebuke, but the people also get a little glimpse of a brighter future.

Chapters 36–39 tell the story of King Hezekiah's illness, which we looked at earlier. They are really a transitional story to show how Assyria gave way to Babylon as the main threat to Judah, through Hezekiah's foolishness in welcoming the envoys from Babylon.

Judah (chapters 1–12 and 24–35)

BAD NEWS

Disobedience

The prophecies of Isaiah were given against a backdrop of peace and prosperity. Indeed, the nation had not known such wealth since the days of Solomon, when the country was at its peak. But alongside the prosperity came pride and indulgence. There was an 'every man for himself' attitude. The poor were oppressed and injustice was common.

The religious life of the nation had become ritualistic. The people went through the routine of worship, but their hearts remained cold towards God. As a result they drifted in their allegiance to God and tolerated pagan idols, worshipping the Canaanite gods Baal and Asherah in the superstitious belief that doing so would make their crops grow and their lives flourish.

Discipline

So a pattern develops similar to the one seen in the Book of Judges. God allows foreign attacks to teach Judah that they should trust in him. As we have seen, these attackers included Syria and Israel, Arabs and Philistines, Edom, Ammon and Moab, and the superpower of Isaiah's early ministry, Assyria (which was eventually defeated by Babylon). But instead of trusting God, they made alliances with whichever power seemed able to provide the most protection at the time. God did not get a look in.

Disaster

God had promised in the time of Moses that if the people did not keep his commands and heed his warnings they would lose the land he had given them. So with Isaiah's warnings falling on deaf ears, in 587 BC the people eventually followed their northern neighbours Israel into exile, though this time at the hands of Babylon.

Dejection

Isaiah predicted that the people's journey and sojourn in Babylon would not be a pleasant one. But he said that it was in exile that many would return to God. As a nation they never again followed after foreign gods. Syncretism and idolatry were banished from their national life.

GOOD NEWS

Remnant

The good news of Part 1 is that from the exile a remnant will return, and that there will be a king who will bring peace to the nations. From the remnant of the people will come a king like David who will be an Everlasting Father, a Counsellor, a Prince of Peace with the government on his shoulder.

Return

It is also clear that despite the disobedience of Judah, God will never break his covenant. So the promise throughout is that they will one day return to the land they had lost. They returned 70 years later, just as Jeremiah would predict.

Reign

Isaiah prophesied that a king would come who would reign like no other. Details of his reign are given: his birth; his ministry in 'Galilee of the Gentiles'; his lineage, from the line of Jesse; his anointing to do God's work. Anyone who doubts the validity of Christ's claim to kingship need only look back to the accuracy of the predictions in Isaiah.

Rejoicing

Throughout the chapters there are times of rejoicing at God's goodness amidst the bad news. See 2:1–5; 12; 14:1–2; 26; 27; 30:19–33; 32:15–20; 34:16–35. Of all the prophetic books, it is Isaiah that is full of joy.

THE NATIONS (CHAPTERS 13–23)

Isaiah mentions a number of nations which had dealings with Judah: Assyria, Babylon, Philistia, Moab, Syria (Damascus), Cush, Egypt, Edom, Arabia and Tyre. There are three points that we should notice:

1 God used them to discipline his people.
2 They exceeded his limits. They were inhuman and unjust, and mocked the God of Israel.
3 God punished them with fire and eventually extinction.

But in spite of this punishment of the nations, Isaiah predicts that the whole earth will share in Judah's blessings (see chapters 23–24).

Part 2 (chapters 40–66)

A picture of God

The second half of Isaiah gives us an incredible picture of God all the way through.

HE'S THE ONLY GOD THERE IS

God says, 'There are no gods beside me.' We are told that the so-called gods don't really exist. God is the only God. Other gods have been invented by the peoples. God also says, 'There are no gods like me.' Isaiah mocks the other gods, pointing out that they have ears but they can't hear, they have eyes but they can't see, they have feet but they can't walk.

This view is, of course, a profoundly offensive statement in our modern world, where we are asked to accept all religions. But there is no God beside the God of Israel.

THE ALMIGHTY CREATOR

The nations are as a drop in the bucket or dust on the scales. It is God who names the stars. Man was commanded by God to name the animals but never to name the stars, and we are wise to remain ignorant of the star sign we were born under. Opinion polls suggest that six out of ten men and seven out of ten women read their horoscope every day. Man should instead look to the Almighty Creator for wisdom about the future.

GOD IS THE HOLY ONE OF ISRAEL

This title for God occurs 25 times in the second part of the Book of Isaiah. Amos focuses on God's righteousness, Hosea on God's faithfulness and Isaiah on God's holiness. It is clear that he never forgot his initial vision of God in his splendour, and so this description becomes a key motif in the book.

THE REDEEMER OF HIS PEOPLE

God is described as the 'kinsman redeemer'. Just as the kinsman redeemer would step in to help a family, so God has the power and is willing to help because of his covenant commitment to his people.

THE SAVIOUR OF THE NATIONS

This title was applied to God in the Book of Isaiah before it was applied to Jesus in the New Testament. It is Isaiah who emphasizes God's concern for all peoples and his desire that there should be an international gathering in the new heaven and earth.

THE LORD OF HISTORY

Isaiah says that the nations are but a drop in the bucket. God begins, controls and ends history. He foretells and controls the future. (See 41:1–6, 21–29; 42:8–9, 10–17; 44:6–8, 25–26; 46:10–11; 48:3.)

ALL FOR HIS GLORY

This focus on God throughout the book is in order that his glory might be made known. The word 'glory' is a key word in the book. God wants his splendour to be displayed for the world to see.

The servant of God

A series of songs are especially significant in the second part of the book and are among its best-known chapters. They are called songs because they are very poetic. They mention a 'servant of God' (20 times), and to this day the Jews don't know who he is.

The meaning of the 'servant' seems to change. On nine occasions the servant seems to be the whole people of Israel (eg. 49:3), but then on other occasions it becomes clear that he is an individual. Furthermore, the title is also given to specific people in other parts of the Old Testament: Uzziah, Josiah, Jeremiah, Ezekiel, Job, Moses and Zerubbabel are all called by this name at various times.

But four things can be said about this servant of the Lord:

1 His faultless character. This servant is perfect; he has no faults. This statement can't be applied to any other person.
2 He is a deeply unhappy man, a man of sorrows who is acquainted with grief.
3 He is executed – killed as a criminal – and yet he is sinless. He is killed for others' sins, not his own. He is accused falsely and his grave is with the rich.
4 After he has been killed for the sins of others, he is raised from the dead and exalted to a very high position.

There is no indication that Isaiah or any other prophet made the connection between the servant of God and the coming king motif earlier in the book. Obviously this is no mystery to the Christian, but to the Jew it is. They can't integrate this servant in the second half of Isaiah with the promised king in the first half. It simply doesn't make sense to them.

The first Jew to make the connection between these two was Jesus, and the connection came at his baptism when God said, 'You are my Son whom I love; with you I am well pleased.' God was putting together something that had been said about the king – 'You are my son' – and something that had been said about the servant – 'With you I am well pleased.' Jesus knew that he was to combine those two figures in one.

Not only did Jesus make the connection, but Peter made it often in his preaching. In the Book of Acts, Peter makes the connection between the king and the servant. Many priests became Christians in the early days because they knew the Book of Isaiah and saw the connection between the king and the servant.

Philip also made the connection when he met the Ethiopian eunuch in the Book of Acts and found that he was reading Isaiah 53.

Paul made the connection supremely. In Philippians he talks about the one who was equal with God and yet took the form of a servant. The Jews don't feel that a king could suffer like that and be put to death as a common criminal. The cross is an offence to the Jewish people – a king nailed to a cross is not the kind of king they want. Jesus doesn't look like the king with the government on his shoulder. They are looking for a victorious king to come and reign, not to die.

The Spirit of God

Perhaps surprisingly, the Holy Spirit is also very prominent in Isaiah. The phrase 'grieving the Holy Spirit' comes from Isaiah 63:10–11. We read that the Spirit anoints this servant for his task (61:1–3). 'I will pour out my Spirit on your offspring' (44:3) – a reference, of course, to Pentecost. We have already noted the reference to 'us' in Isaiah 6, as in 'Whom shall I send and who will go for us?'

So the Trinity is in the Old Testament for those with eyes to see. Here is the mighty God who created the world, here is his suffering servant and here is the Holy Spirit – all three Persons are utterly clear in the second half of Isaiah.

Prophecy

It is important to grasp a principle about understanding prophecy, especially as prophecy comprises a third of the Bible, including 17 books from Isaiah to Malachi. This is especially important with a relatively complicated prophecy such as Isaiah.

All the prophets spoke to their own age and also to the future.

1 **To their own age** It was as if they had a microscope for the present day. They saw their own day clearly through God's eyes and spoke accordingly. But the word's application was not limited to their own day. The abiding moral principles can speak to any culture in any age. For God's character does not change, and his moral standards remain the same for all time.

2 **To the future** They also had a telescope on the future. They spoke of what would happen one day. But this is where it gets complicated, for it was impossible for the prophet to gauge the distance in time between the events he saw, just as someone gazing at mountain peaks from a

long way off would be unable to grasp how much distance there was between them. So what many of the Old Testament prophets (and we as readers) thought was one mountain with two peaks was in fact two mountains spaced far apart. So two future events are described as if they are next to each other, when actually there are thousands of years between them.

Christians today live between the two peaks. One peak is the past and the other peak is the future, because we know something that the prophets didn't know. They looked for the coming of the King, but we know that the King is coming twice.

Not only is this the case, but sometimes the fulfilment of the prophecies does not occur in the order they are given. So we know, for example, that the suffering servant of the second part of Isaiah is fulfilled before the reigning king of the first part. Christ has come as the servant who goes to the cross, but not yet as the king who reigns over all.

So it is not surprising that the Jews who know Isaiah very well are still looking for the first coming. The Jews' expectation that the Messiah would come only once as king caused them to be disillusioned with Jesus, and to disqualify him as their Messiah. When Jesus rode into Jerusalem on Palm Sunday, it seemed that at last he was coming as king, in the way that the crowds wanted him to. They went wild with excitement, thinking he was about to throw the Romans out. But he was riding on a donkey, symbolic of the fact that he hadn't come to fight.

Revelation tells us that when Jesus comes a second time, he will come to fight, for then he comes as a man of war on a white horse. But on Palm Sunday his mission was peace, not to fulfil Isaiah's prophecy of a reigning king. To everyone's amazement, when he came through the gate, he turned left instead of right. To the right was the Roman fortress where the occupying force was based. But Jesus turned to the Temple and whipped the Jews out of it. His priorities were different from those of the Jews.

So we can perhaps imagine why, a few days later, the same crowd said, 'Crucify him!' and chose to save Barabbas, the guerrilla fighter, instead. They thought he was coming to take the throne, but all he did was clean up the Temple – how very disappointing! So when Pilate placed a plaque above his head reading 'This is the king of the Jews' they couldn't believe it. The only man in that whole nation who believed it said, 'Lord, remember me when you get your kingdom.' For the dying thief saw in the suffering, dying man One who was the coming king.

The ultimate future

INTERNATIONAL

We have noted already that the message of Isaiah, especially of the second part, is that the whole earth would know God's blessings, not just the Jews. He mentions that 'distant islands' will know God. It is likely that this is a reference to Britain, since this land was referred to as a 'distant island' by the Phoenicians, who shipped tin from the Cornish mines.

NATIONAL

Yet this worldwide focus does not mean that Judah is forgotten. Jerusalem, Zion and the mountains of the Lord are to be the location of God's activity too. We know that one day he will come on a horse and take over the governments of the world. The kingdoms of this world will become the Kingdom of our God and of his Christ. So the Church today is getting people ready for the king to come and reign. We are preparing sub-jects in all nations now so that he can come back. When the good news is preached to all the nations, then the end shall come, because God wants all ethnic groups to be represented.

In the second part of Isaiah it seems as if he is constantly switching from the future of Jerusalem to the future of the nations. But we also find in Isaiah 4 that the house of the Lord will be established on the mountains, and all the nations will come to it. It's a future for a 'united nations', but it is centred on Jerusalem. Just as the suffering servant element has happened, so will the reigning king element.

So why do we read Isaiah?

1 It's part of God's word. The study of any part of the Scriptures is able to make us 'wise unto salvation'. In Isaiah the key words are 'save' and 'salvation' (the name Isaiah itself means 'God saves').

2 The book is a good introduction to the whole Bible. It is a summary of all the themes of both Testaments, brought into one book by the Spirit's inspiration. So if you think the Bible is too big a book for you to read through, read Isaiah for a start, and it will introduce you to all the themes of Scripture.

3 It is a very good introduction to prophecy. It is in one of the three Major Prophets, placed first in the section of the prophets in our Bible. It is typical of most prophecy in being a combination of protest about the present and prediction about the future. It is easy to see the ways in which certain parts are fulfilled by Christ's coming in the New Testament.

4 Isaiah helps us to link the Old and New Testaments by showing us how they illuminate each other. We can understand the New Testament much better if we know Isaiah.

5 We read it to get to know Jesus. Jesus said, 'Search the
   Scriptures, for they bear testimony to me.' He's talking
   about the Old Testament. Isaiah helps the reader to understand the Lord better than almost any other Old Testament
   book. If you read through Isaiah 53, you are at the foot of
   the cross. 'By his stripes we are healed.'

6 We gain a bigger view of God. 'O magnify the Lord with
   me' means 'Enlarge your understanding of God himself.'
   The second half of Isaiah gives us a bigger view of God, the
   Holy One of Israel, the Creator of the ends of the earth.

Thus, although Isaiah is the largest prophetic book, and will
take time and effort to be understood, there are many reasons
why Christians should make it the one prophetic book that
they definitely read.

It is the Bible in miniature. It will aid their understanding
of the Old Testament, illuminate their understanding of the
New and, most importantly, enlarge their vision of God.

PART V

MICAH

Introduction

The prophetic books from Hosea to Malachi are called the 'Minor Prophets' in our Bibles. But this is a misnomer, for it suggests that one group is lesser than the other. In fact, they were so called to distinguish the smaller books from the larger three – that is, Isaiah, Jeremiah and Ezekiel. This misnomer is never more so than with the prophecy of Micah. For he has a memorable message – one that still reverberates around the world today.

Micah was a contemporary of Isaiah, and one section of the Book of Micah is identical to a section in the Book of Isaiah. It concerns beating swords into plough-shares and spears into pruning-hooks, and the reign of peace that will come when Christ returns. Who copied whom, or whether the Holy Spirit gave them an identical message is unclear, but they were both speaking to the same situation, so it's clear that God wanted the same message to be given again.

There is a passage from Micah which you will have heard read at carol services: 'But you, Bethlehem Ephrathah, though you are small among the clans of Judah, out of you will come for me one who will be ruler over Israel' (5:2). The prediction was made 700 years before Jesus was born.

There is a classic verse: 'He has showed you, O man, what is good. And what does the Lord require of you? To act justly and to love mercy and to walk humbly with your God' (6:8), and there is a statement right at the end of the book which has been made into a number of hymns: 'Who is a pardoning God like you?' (7:18).

These are all memorable, but they are usually taken out of context and used as pretexts. We must put the whole book into context, into time and place. God always expressed his word at a particular time and to a particular place. That is why the Bible, unlike all other holy books in the world, is full of history and geography. If you read the Koran or the Hindu Vedas you will find that they are just books of thoughts and words. But the Bible is a book of history and geography, because God unfolded his total revelation at particular times and in particular places, and this is very important for Micah.

Where?

The promised land was a very narrow strip between the Mediterranean on the one hand and the Arabian Desert on the other. It was a corridor through which all the traffic from Europe, Asia and Africa had to pass. It usually passed down the coast along a road called the Way of the Sea. The crossroads of the world was at the hill of Megiddo (Armageddon in Hebrew). All the world's traffic passed through it, and there was a little village called Nazareth on a hill overlooking the crossroads. For this reason Galilee, the northern part of Israel, was called 'Galilee of the Nations', because international traffic went through it. The south was far more culturally Jewish. It was up in the hills with far fewer international visitors.

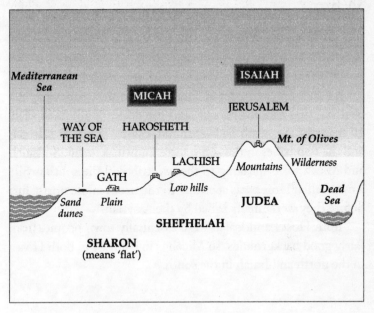

If you take an east-west cross-section in the south, we have the Mediterranean Sea at one side and the Dead Sea at the other. The Dead Sea is a lot lower than the Mediterranean.

Micah came from the Shephelah, a district of hills 20 miles inland on a 3,000-metre shelf. He lived between the Philistines and the Jews. As such he could look up to the corrupt city of Jerusalem and down to the Gaza Strip.

A key detail to appreciate is that Isaiah and Micah were contemporaries. They were preaching at the same time, but Isaiah was born in the royal palace. He was a cousin of the king and so was comfortable conversing with the government. Micah, by contrast, lived in the Shephelah, a poor region. So Isaiah came from an upper-class, wealthy background, but Micah was a simple country man with a heart for the ordinary people who were being exploited. By reason of his background, Isaiah was not so conscious of this, so they complement each other very neatly.

When?

It is probable that Micah prophesied around 735 BC, when the bad King Ahaz was on the throne (735–715), though it is also possible that his work overlapped with an earlier king, Jotham.

By this time, of course, Israel was divided, following the civil war that had broken out after the death of Solomon. The 10 tribes of the north had separated, calling themselves Israel, and the two tribes in the south were known as Judah. So Isaiah and Micah were speaking to the two tribes in the south, while a man called Hosea was speaking to the tribes in the north, just before they were finally exiled by the Assyrians.

Both Hosea and Isaiah were essentially town people, from fairly good backgrounds, so Micah is in contrast to both Hosea in the north and Isaiah in the south.

Why?

King Jotham (750–731) and King Ahaz had led the country astray. Jotham was regarded as a 'good' king, but he failed to remove the 'high places' from the land. These high places encouraged the worship of the Canaanite gods. The king should have upheld the Law of God and made sure that the people did the same. Ahaz, however, was a 'bad' king and failed to stop the evil practices that were spreading from the north-ern ten tribes to the southern two, and from the cities to the country. In the Bible cities are always seen as dangerous envi-ronments. The concentration of sinners accentuates the spread of sin. So vice and crime are normally worse in the city than in the surrounding country.

In the case of Judah, the corruption in Jerusalem was beginning to touch the country towns in the Shephelah. Micah could see the effect that the bad influence was having, and it hurt him. He observed bribery among the judges, the prophets and the priests. The very people who should have upheld the Law of God were being paid to say things that the people wanted to hear. There was exploitation of the powerless. Covetousness, greed, cheating, violence and cruelty became all too common. Crime was on the increase; landlords were stealing from the poor, evicting widows and orphans and putting them out on the streets; merchants and traders were using inaccurate scales and weights, so that business was corrupt. Sin was infiltrating every level of society. Above all, the rich and powerful were abusing the poor. Social and political power were being used to line pockets. It is a sad picture – a complete breakdown of respect and trust. Family relationships, the mainstay of any nation, were disintegrating. But Micah had a passion for social justice and was horrified that such things were happening among God's people – a people who were intended to be a light to the nations.

Amidst his concern about the situation, Micah had a vision from God that touched Judah, the north and the surrounding nations. His vision seemed to go out in ripples. His first vision was really for the tribe of Judah, and then his vision went further afield and he had a vision for the whole nation – even those 10 tribes in the north, though they would now have nothing to do with the south. His heart was enlarged to carry the burden of the lost world, though it started with a burden for his own people.

He saw God coming down to deal with Judah. He would judge them and take away from them even their little bit of land in the south. It was a painful thing to see, and it affected him very deeply.

There were two factors which made him feel all this: one was the Holy Spirit and one was his own spirit. Every prophet had a dynamic encounter with the Holy Spirit that led him to preach. But often his human spirit also felt the pain. Micah said that he howled like a jackal and cried like an ostrich and tore off his clothes, so great was his anguish. He realized that the situation was hopeless.

He was especially concerned about three problems: idolatry, immorality and injustice. It was injustice that was really getting to his heart. He couldn't bear to see what God's people were doing to each other. Idolatry is when people insult God and worship something else. Immorality is when people indulge themselves. But injustice is when people injure each other, and this was the biggest burden in his heart. As 'one of the people', his heart went out to the widows and orphans who were on the street because they couldn't pay the rent. There is a strong cry for social justice throughout his prophecy.

I always find it helpful to see the structure and shape of a book, especially if it is as well ordered as the Book of Micah. It is in three quite distinct parts. I have given them different titles to indicate the main thrust of each part.

Chapters 1–3 simply talk about crime and punishment – the bad things that are happening which God is going to punish. Chapters 4–5 focus on peace and security. Justice and mercy are the themes of chapters 6–7.

Crime and punishment (chapters 1–3)

In these chapters Micah is urging the people to grasp that sin has now spread from the city even to the country villages and towns in the Shephelah where he came from. The content of his message cleverly grabs their attention. He pronounces judgement on them by using the name of each village in a way that means they would never forget his message.

The places

If Micah were preaching in London, he would say something like this: 'Hackney will be hacked to pieces. Hammersmith will be hammered flat. Battersea will be battered for all to see and Shoreditch will be thrown in a ditch near the shore. Crouch End will crouch with fear at the end and there will be no healing for Ealing. Harrow will find itself under a harrow and Church End will see the end of the Church. Barking will be set on by wild dogs and sheep will graze over what is left of Shepherd's Bush. Vultures will feed on the corpses at Peckham.'

It may sound a bit odd to write in this way, but that is exactly how Micah speaks about local places. He takes every village name in the Shephelah and he twists that name to be a message of judgement. It is a brilliant bit of preaching to show that God won't let them get away with their behaviour. Sooner or later he will do something about it.

The people

It is clear that God held the influential leaders responsible for the situation. He pointed the finger at the king, the priests and the false prophets who had allowed the spiritual decay to develop unhindered. But he was especially concerned about the profiteers whose ruthless exploitation of the weak meant that the rich got richer and the poor got poorer.

Peace and security (chapters 4–5)

Chapters 4–5 are a surprise, for they contain mostly good news. Chapter 3 ends with Jerusalem in ruins. Micah says that the instigator of the sin – the big city – will be laid waste. But in chapters 4–5 we have a different picture. He is saying that the present corrupt state is not the end of the story.

The Kingdom

A Kingdom is coming in which there will be multilateral disarmament – all disputes will be settled by a King in Zion. The headquarters of the United Nations should not be in New York, but in Jerusalem, for that is where disputes will one day be settled. When 'the Lord reigns in Zion' he will settle all the world's disputes. The Kingdom is going to be established on earth. When we pray the Lord's Prayer, we pray for this to happen: 'Your Kingdom come on earth, as it is in heaven.' Of course, it can't come until the King comes, because you can't have a Kingdom without a King. Micah went on to say that the King is going to come from the little village of Bethlehem. *Beth* means 'house' and *lehem* means 'bread', so the name literally means 'house of bread'. It was this little village that supplied corn to Jerusalem, as well as lambs for sacrifice.

The King

Micah looks ahead, not just to Jesus' first coming, but to his second. The description is of his second coming, when he comes to reign on earth over the nations. The wording is identical to Isaiah 2:1–4, raising the question of which came first. Did one copy the other, did they both copy from someone else, or did they receive identical messages from God? It is impossible to tell with any certainty.

So the whole of the second part of Micah is good news. The city of David will supply the King who will come to rule the world and bring peace and prosperity.

Justice and mercy (chapters 6–7)

The last section of Micah is in the form of a court scene. God is the counsel for the prosecution and Micah is the counsel for the defence. The people of Judah, now corrupted by sin, are standing in the dock and God is vindicating himself.

God speaks in the personal pronoun, 'I', and so does Micah. They have an argument about who is in the dock. God explains that what he really wanted from them was not sacrifices (the blood of thousands of lambs), but righteousness. He said he required them to 'act justly, love mercy and walk humbly before God'.

Justice is giving people what they deserve, but mercy is giving them what they don't deserve. A man was having his portrait painted and said to the artist, 'I hope this will do me justice.' The artist said, 'It is not justice you need, it is mercy!'

Justice and mercy are not contradictory; they travel the same road together. The difference is that justice can only go so far, but mercy takes over and goes further, and God is the supreme master of both. God will always do justly. No one will ever be able to say that God is unfair.

But all that God received was the blood of thousands of lambs. Judah kept up the ritual and the religious side, but God was looking for more than that. The one thing that matters is how men stand with God, and the one test of that is how they stand with man. If you are in relationship with God, then you will find yourself acting justly and showing mercy, because that is exactly how he acts towards you.

Micah is miserable in the court scene, and then his misery gives way to rejoicing when he realizes that the judge in the courtroom is going to show mercy as well. So we get this lovely balance at the end of the book, with the covenant of mercy that God makes.

When a child is naughty a parent has a problem. Are you going to show them justice and give them what they deserve or let them off? It is very hard to be just and merciful, except under one circumstance, and that is where an innocent person is prepared to suffer the justice on behalf of the guilty. Then sin can be punished and pardoned at the same time. That is why the cross was necessary. As the hymn 'Beneath the Cross of Jesus' puts it:

> O safe and happy shelter,
> O refuge tried and sweet,
>   O trysting place
> Where heaven's love and
>   Heaven's justice meet.
>
> *Elizabeth Cecilia Clephane (1830-65)*

At the cross we see God's perfect justice (the death penalty for sin is exacted) and also God's perfect mercy (that the guilty can go free), because the innocent has paid the price. If God forgave us without the cross, then he would be merciful but not just. If he refused to forgive sin and punished it all, he would be just but he wouldn't be merciful. This is why the Old Testament background is so important. We learn that the Israelites knew forgiveness of sin through the sacrifice of an innocent life. Without shedding of blood there can be no forgiveness of sin, because if there is no shedding of blood, then God cannot be both just and merciful.

Micah also writes of the need to 'walk humbly'. This third requirement is just as important as the other two. It is possible to do the first two and feel proud, but you are only doing it because God first did it for you, and you walk humbly with him.

In the New Testament Matthew picks up the prediction that a ruler would come from Bethlehem. A decision made by the Roman Emperor in his palace in Rome, thousands of miles away, brought Joseph and Mary to Bethlehem to pay their poll tax. It was amazing timing.

But the New Testament also tells us that when that King comes, he will take over the government of the world and bring peace to all the earth. This has yet to be fulfilled, but it will happen when Christ comes again.

It is important to note that there are many prophecies explaining what will happen when the Messiah comes which were not fulfilled when Jesus came the first time. This is a great offence to the Jewish people. They believe that the Messiah will bring worldwide peace, and so because Jesus failed to do this, he cannot be the Messiah. But a secret hidden from all the prophets of the Old Testament and only revealed in the New was that the Messiah would come twice – first to die for our sins and secondly to rule the world.

Theological themes

Before leaving Micah we would do well to highlight some of the theological themes present in the book.

Two sides of God's character

It depicts two sides of God's character: he is just and so must punish, but he is merciful and so can pardon. He hates sin, but loves sinners. This theme permeates the book. Each section begins with condemnation and ends with consolation. So justice comes before mercy. Sin must be punished before it is pardoned.

Micah reminds us that we should leave the work to God. We must reflect God but not replace him. But our job today is still to 'act justly, love mercy and walk humbly before God.' That requirement will never change.

Where Christ will come

The prophecy tells us clearly that the King will come to Bethlehem, a most unlikely place. It was small and insignificant, apart from its provision of bread for the Jerusalem market and lambs for the Temple sacrifices. But the prophecy was fulfilled, and all through the poll tax of Caesar Augustus.

Why Christ will come

The prophecy also points forward to Jesus' second coming, when he will rule over the whole world. So prophecies that were not fulfilled in his first coming will be fulfilled when he comes a second time.

Social action

The prophecy also gives Christians a charter for our life in society. The Church should have a prophetic voice, alerting people to the evils of exploitation where they occur and providing a voice for the poor and disadvantaged. In so doing we are preparing for the time when we will reign with Christ when he returns.

Social rejection

In view of this, Christians should not be surprised when those around them, even those close to them, dislike what they stand for. Micah himself said that 'a man's enemies are the members of his own household.' Jesus told his disciples that just as some people hated him, so they would hate his disciples also. Christians today must be prepared to walk as he did and face the consequences.

PART VI

NAHUM

Introduction

The prophet Nahum is closely linked with his better-known colleague Jonah, so when we looked at Jonah we noted the similarities between them. They both came from the 10 tribes of the north and were both sent to Nineveh, the capital of Assyria, the major world power. However, Nahum's message of destruction came 150 years after Jonah's time, when the circumstances were very different.

The recent history was as follows: after Jonah went to Nineveh, Assyria's empire expanded. They tried to invade the 10 tribes of the north during King Ahab's reign, but they failed. They came back during the reign of the Assryian king Ashurbanipal III and took the tribe of Benjamin away completely, only to return later under Shalmaneser to deport the other tribes into exile. From that point on, all that was left of the land was little Judah in the south. It was a catastrophic time for the people of God.

During Hezekiah's reign Sennacherib came and besieged Jerusalem, but was repulsed when an angel killed 185,000 Assyrians. But they were not deterred and continued their expansion. They conquered Thebes in Upper Egypt and became a mighty empire.

Following Jonah, two prophets were given messages for Assyria. First Zephaniah, as part of his message to Judah, predicted that God would destroy Assyria and make its great capital Nineveh a desolate wasteland. The once-proud city would become a pastureland for sheep and a variety of wild animals would make their homes there. Once-great palaces would lie in ruins, open to the elements.

But Zephaniah spoke of this destruction without specifying when it would happen. It was Nahum who finally told the Assyrians that they were finished. In his prophecy we have the record of their final warning. The one big difference between Jonah and Nahum is that on this occasion, God did not let them off. It is interesting that they both describe God as slow to anger, but the difference with Nahum was that time had run out. Once God's anger is aroused, you cannot turn it away. While his wrath is simmering it can be turned away, but when it boils over, nothing can stop it. There is, of course, a day coming when the whole world will face God's wrath. We read in Revelation of a day when people would rather be swallowed in an earthquake than look at the anger on the face of God.

The king of Nineveh prayed and fasted again, as at the time of Jonah, but God would not accept it. It was too late to change. The last verse of Nahum has the stern words: 'There is no remedy for your wound; your injury is past healing.'

Amazingly, this is described as good news – though not, of course, for the Assyrians. It is good news for Israel and for Nahum, who was born under Assyrian rule in the Holy Land. Nahum is telling the Assyrians that everyone who hears the news about their downfall will clap their hands, 'for who has not felt your endless cruelty?' It is a vivid prophecy.

As with the prophecy of Jonah, there is a question that underlies the Book of Nahum which has troubled Christians down through the generations. The prophecy of Jonah asks,

'Does God control nature?' Nahum asks, 'Does God control history?' The Bible says it is God who draws the atlas of history. When the apostle Paul preached to the Greeks on Mars Hill at Athens, he said that God allots every nation its place in time and space. God allows a nation to rise and become an empire, and it is God who brings it to an end. I believe that God brought the British empire to an end when we washed our hands of the Jewish people in 1947 and said we wanted nothing more to do with the Jews. Within five years the empire had gone.

God not only controls all of nature, he also controls all of history. It is he who raises up princes and brings them down. God is in charge of history, and therefore history is predictable. Part of the prophets' task was to predict history – to write history before it happened. Nahum is saying that Nineveh is finished, which seems unbelievable when you look at the power and might of Nineveh.

An outline of the book

Below is an outline of Nahum's prophecy. It has only three chapters and divides easily between them. Their focus is the fall of Nineveh.

Proclamation – Who? – Intervention (chapter 1)
Disaster for his enemies
Deliverance for his friends

Description – How? – Invasion (chapter 2)
A day of looting
A day of lions

Explanation – Why? – Inhumanity (chapter 3)
Conquest by force
Corruption by finance

Proclamation (chapter 1)

First of all there is the proclamation that God's enemies are going to be punished by him. Divine intervention means disaster for God's enemies, and deliverance for his friends. God's intervention always has this dual character. When he steps into history and acts, it means disaster for all those who defy God and who trust themselves. God is a jealous God. He is not envious – God doesn't envy anybody anything, because it's all his anyway – but he is jealous. Envy is wanting what someone else has; jealousy is wanting what's rightfully yours. You may be envious about someone else's wife, but you would be jealous about your own. So God is jealous for his name, his reputation, his people, and his world. God says, 'It's my name, it's my reputation, it's my world, and I won't allow people to behave like this in my world.'

Alongside God's jealousy is his vengeance. These are not popular attributes of God, but we need to understand them if we are to gain a proper appreciation of who he is. Nahum concentrates almost exclusively on God's jealousy and vengeance against those who defy him and trust themselves.

The first chapter is an acrostic poem, where each verse begins with the next letter of the Hebrew alphabet, and so is easily remembered by the people of Israel. It was good news for them – something to store in their hearts.

Chapter 1 alternates between a statement to Nineveh and a statement to Israel – bad news for one and good news for the other. It is a marvellous literary work. Nahum could put words together in a memorable way, by the inspiration of the Holy Spirit.

Description (chapter 2)

If chapter 1 is a proclamation that Nineveh will fall, chapter 2 is a description of how it will happen. It is absolutely astonishing in its detail – almost as if Nahum was watching the events unfold on television.

The fascinating thing is that the people who came to destroy Nineveh wore scarlet uniforms, just as Nahum had prophesied, even though such uniforms were unheard of in Nahum's day. He saw too how they entered through the river gates and described the city of blood:

> Listen, I hear the crack of the whips as the chariots rush forward against her. Wheels rumbling, horses' hooves pounding and chariots clattering as they bump wildly through the streets. See the flashing swords and glittering spears in the upraised hands of the cavalry. The dead are lying in the streets – bodies, heaps of bodies, everywhere. Men stumble over them, scramble to their feet and fall again.
>
> All this because Nineveh sold herself to the enemies of God.

It is vivid writing, and we can imagine the prophet preaching it. Nahum was calling Nineveh a toothless lion – an aptly chosen picture, because the lion was the emblem of Assyria. But they are no longer a threat to anyone and are in terror themselves. So there's a kind of poetic justice in this.

Explanation (chapter 3)

In chapter 3 Nahum moves from description to explanation. The reason for judgement is the sheer inhumanity of Assyria. We see here God's justice. He doesn't judge the Assyrians for breaking the Ten Commandments, because they don't know them. When God sends a prophet to pronounce against people who are not the people of God, he accuses them of the crimes against humanity that they know instinctively are wrong. Those who have never heard of the Ten Commandments still know that it's wrong to be barbaric and cruel.

So God judges people by what they know. This is a principle that goes right through Scripture. If a person doesn't know the Ten Commandments, they will not be judged for breaking them. If a person has never heard of Christ, they will not be judged for not having heard of Christ. But everybody has some knowledge of God through the creation around them and their conscience inside them. God will judge everyone by what they know instinctively to be wrong. So the United Nations document U144, the Declaration of Human Rights, wasn't written by Christians, but it includes the sort of things that all would acknowledge as just and right.

So God was judging the Assyrians' evil practices. In their chariots they would ride all over a country, slaughtering all the inhabitants and taking it by force. They were also corrupted by money, and bribery was common among them. Nahum said they knew that these two things were wrong, and because of them God was going to destroy their city.

I find that remarkable, because our world is not a stranger to either of these sins, and people know they are both wrong.

What happened to Nineveh?

Today Nineveh is a desert. The once-great palace is completely gone. In its place live owls and hedgehogs and all the wild beasts, just as predicted by Zephaniah. It was lost for centuries, but was found by an Englishman called Layard in 1820 on the west bank of the Tigris.

What happened to Nahum?

We know that the prophet never returned from Nineveh. His tomb can be found on the west bank of the Tigris today. It is revered by the Arabs, who recognize Nahum as one of the holy men of God.

Capernaum, a town in Galilee, was named after him (*Caper* = 'village', *naum* = 'Nahum'). It was this village, among others, that received the condemnation of Jesus. As with Nineveh, they too refused to hear the word of the Lord. Like the once-great city, Capernaum also lies in rubble today.

PART VII

ZEPHANIAH

The messenger (1:1)

The prophetic books focus more on the message than on the messenger, and this is never more true than with Zephaniah. We know very little about him. The only biographical details are in verse 1 of chapter 1, where we are told his name and his genealogy. The name Zephaniah in Hebrew is *Sephenjah*, which means 'hidden God'. It is uncertain whether this means God had hidden himself or if Zephaniah had been hidden by God. His genealogy gives us a clue, for he is the only prophet who traces his ancestry back four generations. Hezekiah, the last 'good' king of Judah (see Isaiah 36–39), was his great-grandfather. So Zephaniah was of royal blood. During Manasseh's reign, royal offspring were being sacrificed to the god Molech under the king's direction, so it is my theory that Zephaniah was hidden by his mother so that he would avoid the slaughter. Hence his very name is a reflection of God's preservation of him to be a prophet for the people.

The genealogy gives us the era in which he lived and preached. Since the time of Hezekiah, the nation had drifted away from God. In addition to child sacrifice and the worship of Molech, Manasseh reinstated the phallic symbols and asherah poles on the high ground and encouraged the people to go back to the fertility cults, with their sexual overtones. The site for child sacrifice was Gehennah, a valley just south of Jerusalem, cursed by Jeremiah and used as a picture of hell by Jesus. Throughout the early years of Manasseh's reign Isaiah tried to stop the decline in national morality and warned Manasseh of the dire consequences of his evil ways. But the king refused to listen and forbade Isaiah to preach, so that he had to write down his prophecies and circulate them in written form. Eventually Manasseh ordered Isaiah's execution.

That wasn't all, for Manasseh was also involved with astrology and spiritualist mediums, in further defiance of the Law of God. This spiritual confusion led to moral chaos, for idolatory always leads to immorality. God's verdict on Manasseh in 2 Chronicles was that he was more evil than the original Canaanites – a staggering statement, given that God had instructed his people to expel the Canaanites because of their corrupt lives. So we can imagine how God felt at this point. He had removed the evil Canaanites to make room for his holy people, and now they were worse than the people they had replaced.

Manasseh died after reigning for 55 years and was succeeded by Amon, a very weak character who did nothing to put the situation right, and Judah continued to slide. Amon was assassinated after only two years on the throne. The whole nation was in moral chaos.

Then an eight-year-old boy named Josiah became king, though the real ruler in the early years was Hilkiah, the High Priest. With good and bad kings in his family tree, it was not clear who this boy king would follow – Hezekiah, his great-grandfather, or Manasseh, his grandfather. So God sent Zephaniah the prophet to prevent the nation from being exiled for their sin, as their northern brothers had been.

The message (1:2–3)

The voice of prophecy had been silent for 70 years. Ever since the death of Hezekiah and the murder of Isaiah there had been no word from God. So Zephaniah spoke into a vacuum with a very strong message.

The prophecy has been called the compendium of all prophecy, because it includes so many elements also found in other prophets' work. His whole message revolved around the 'Day of the Lord', which is mentioned 23 times in the prophecy. This 'Day' is not a 24-hour period but means an era of time, as in 'the day of the horse and cart'. It was the day of God's judgement, of putting things right; the day of the vindication of righteousness, when wrongs were righted and wickedness was punished.

There is a parallel in the English calendar. Historically, there are four quarter days for settling accounts: Lady Day (25 March), Midsummer Day (24 June), Michaelmas Day (29 September) and Christmas Day (25 December). All accounts were examined, audited and settled, and fraud was punished. They give us a picture of the Day of the Lord.

Zephaniah uses an interesting word to describe God's emotions. He says that God is 'irritated', though with none of the selfish petulance that humans exhibit. The Day of the Lord is the day when God has had enough and his anger boils over.

There are two sorts of anger in the Bible. One is the inner anger that a person keeps inside and doesn't let out. It simmers away and is not obvious to other people. The other is the anger that erupts suddenly so that everyone knows. So it is this inner anger that is demonstrated in the Book of Zephaniah. The prophet is saying that God's anger is simmering now, and the day of wrath will come, when God can't hold it in any longer.

Although simmering anger is often missed, the signs that God is angry can be seen. The symptoms of the simmering are there for all to see in a society going downhill (compare Romans 1). But one day God's anger is going to boil over. We must put off this day by repenting and getting things put right. This is one of the themes of the prophecy.

An outline of the Book of Zephaniah

Foreign religion (1:4–2:3)
Deserved (1:4–6)
Declared (1:7–9)
Described (1:10–16)
Deflected (2:1–3)

Foredoomed regions (2:4–15)
The west – Philistia (2:4–7)
The east – Moab and Ammon (2:8–11)
The south – Egypt and Ethiopia (2:12)
The north – Assyria (2:13–15)

Future redemption (3:1–20)
Curses – divine justice (3:1–8)
  (a) National obstinacy (3:1–7)
    (i) Rebelling (3:1–4)
    (ii) Resisting (3:5–7)
  (b) International obliteration (3:8)

Blessings – divine mercy (3:9–20)
  (a) International godliness (3:9)
  (b) National gladness (3:10–20)
    (i) Rejoicing (3:10–17)
    (ii) Returning (3:18–20)

These three sections are very clear, but as is often the case, the chapter headings don't divide the book appropriately.

Foreign religion (1:4–2:3)

In the first section the prophet is concerned with the foreign religions which have become part of Judah's national life. He announces judgement and makes four basic statements about the Day of the Lord that is coming.

Deserved (1:4–6)

There had been considerable drift away from a proper relationship with God. Many had abandoned their allegiance to the God of Israel in favour of other gods. The priests, who should have been ensuring that the covenant was kept, were themselves leading people astray. Superstition was common and many followed Manasseh's evil worship of Molech.

Declared (1:6–9)

Zephaniah describes what will happen to them when God judges them. When we read the prophetic books we may feel we are reading exactly the same message. But God needs to repeat himself, especially as there have been 70 years between these words and his last ones. Zephaniah is warning the people that the Day when the Lord will judge is coming very close.

Described (1:10–17)

The judgement will be catastrophic for the people. They are largely complacent about their behaviour and how God feels about it. Zephaniah warns them that when the judgement comes, everyone will know.

Deflected (2:1–3)

He then offers them the possibility that even at this stage, judgement can be deflected from Israel and turned away by repentance. It is the same message that all the prophets have. If they will humble themselves, God will hear and forgive and show them mercy in return. Indeed, the need for meekness is a key requirement in the prophets' messages (see Isaiah 2:9 and Micah 6:8).

Foredoomed regions (2:4–15)

Zephaniah addresses the nations threatening Judah from every point of the compass. On the west side of Judah was the land of Philistia, from which modern 'Palestine' claims to be descended. On the east side were Moab and Ammon, and to the south were Egypt and Ethiopia. To the north-east was Assyria, the world power of the day, on the Tigris and Euphrates rivers. Few nations were unaffected by the Assyrians. They had taken away the 10 tribes in the north. Babylon at this stage was still a small and insignificant power.

Zephaniah is given a message that these nations will be judged by God. God is the judge of the whole world, and they will be judged for their attitude to Judah. But this interaction with Judah is a two-way one. Not only does God judge foreign nations for their attitude to Judah, but he also uses them to discipline Judah. We are told in the Book of Amos that God brought the Philistines from Crete to inhabit the land west of Canaan at the same time as the children of Israel invaded Canaan. It is God who moves nations around and draws the map to dictate where people will be.

So the Philistines became a real thorn in the side of Israel, right through to the time of King David (about 700 years later).

Indeed, the name 'Philistine' has become proverbial in the English language to describe someone who is hostile to other cultures. In Deuteronomy God explains the situation: 'I have brought them to test you. If you keep my word, you will keep them at bay and they will be no problem to you. But if you disobey me, I have brought them to be an instrument of discipline for you, and when you are doing wrong they will overcome you.'

This action demonstrates God's concern. God is a Father to his people, and a good father disciplines his children when they go wrong. In fact, Hebrews 12 says, 'If the Lord doesn't discipline you, then you are not a true son of God.' This principle is not always grasped by Bible readers. If you become a child of God, then God will discipline you when you sin. But God does this so that you won't need to be punished after death. So Christians can expect life in this world to be tough. I can never believe the testimonies in which people claim that after they came to Jesus all their troubles disappeared. I believed them once, but it depressed me, for my testimony was so different. I came to Jesus, and my troubles began! When I was baptized in the Spirit my troubles became even worse. I have been in more trouble in the last five years than in the previous 40! But I am glad, because it fits the promises of Jesus. He said, 'In the world you will have big troubles. But cheer up – I am on top of them!'

Future redemption (3:1–20)

In the last section there is a strange tension between cursing and blessing. It is almost as if Zephaniah is saying, 'Choose what you really want to have. Do you really want God's justice?' He is full of mercy and wants to have mercy on us, but he can't give it without our cooperation, because he only gives to those who ask for it.

I listen to many prayers for all kinds of things, but it thrills me to hear people ask for mercy, for they have understood a key law of the Kingdom. We only ask for mercy if we think we are bad. If we think we are fine, we ask for health, strength, guidance, all sorts of things – but we never ask for mercy.

Curses – divine justice (3:1–8)

(A) NATIONAL OBSTINACY (3:1–7)

(i) Rebelling (3:1–4)

In the first half of chapter 3 Zephaniah faces the people with the possibility of a day of divine justice, when he tells them how obstinate they are. They have rebelled against God quite deliberately and are resistant to God's appeal.

(ii) Resisting (3:5–7)

He also accuses them of resistance. The rulers, officials, priests and prophets are all implicated. They are an obstinate people. A while ago, having read the verse in Zephaniah, 'Morning by morning he dispenses justice', I composed a song of my own, to the tune of the hymn 'Great is thy faithfulness':

> Great is thy righteousness,
> O God all holy.
> There is no error of judgement with thee.
> Thou changest not, thy commandments
> They fade not.
> As thou hast been, thou for ever wilt be.

Great is thy righteousness,
Great is thy righteousness,
Morning by morning thy justice I see.
All that is merited
Thou has requited.
Great is thy righteousness –
Lord, hear our plea.

We love to sing pleasant songs about God's positive attributes such as faithfulness, but we must accept that there is another side to God, and we should be grateful for that too. Paul says in his Letter to the Romans that we should 'Consider the kindness and sternness of God – sternness to those who fell but kindness to you, providing you continue in his kindness.'

Zephaniah is telling the people that if they continue rebelling and resisting there will be a national disaster. God's anger will boil over and the Day of the Lord will come.

(B) INTERNATIONAL OBLITERATION (3:8)

What is true of God's anger towards Judah is also true of the whole world. He says that this same anger will boil over towards the nations and wipe them out. They will all stand before him and the wicked will be consumed by his jealous anger.

Blessings – divine mercy (3:9–20)

The book concludes with a note of hope, in common with many of the prophets. For example, Amos preached a message of God's justice, as the penultimate prophet to the 10 tribes in the north before they disappeared, but the last word to the north was the prophecy of Hosea, a message of God's mercy and love. It is almost as if God's last word to us is 'Won't you have my mercy?' Zephaniah finishes in the same way. God doesn't want to punish – he has no pleasure in the death of the wicked. He wants to show mercy, and so finishes on a note of hope for the future.

(A) INTERNATIONAL GODLINESS (3:9)

His note of mercy for the nations is that out of every nation he will draw people who love him. We are told that people will come out of every kindred, tribe, tongue and nation. God doesn't want a single ethnic group on earth to be missed out. This is why he told us to preach the gospel to all ethnic groups and to make disciples of them.

(B) NATIONAL GLADNESS (3:10–20)

But then he finishes up with the possibilities of blessing for Israel itself. Nine times in this last little section God says 'I will …' Judah may break his covenant, but he will never break it.

(i) Rejoicing (3:10–17).

In that day no one will be proud or haughty; they will do no one wrong and tell no lies. No one will be able to make them afraid. He talks about a wonderful future when he will quiet them with his love. He even says God will sing about his people: 'he will rejoice over them with singing'.

(ii) Returning (3:18–20).

God will gather those who have been scattered and bring home a remnant who will revere his name. Though they have been despised, they will be exalted in the eyes of the world. God will give them 'praise and honour in every land where they were put to shame'. So at the end of the book there is a note of extraordinary hope. God's people have the opportunity to be judged now and to get right with God now.

Conclusion

We are left with one question about Zephaniah. Was Zephaniah's prophecy effective? Did Josiah take any notice?

Josiah came to the throne at the age of eight in 640 BC and reigned for 31 years. At first he was heavily influenced by the High Priest, Hilkiah, who tended to keep the status quo, but then he began to be influenced by Zephaniah. At the age of 16 he destroyed the altars in Jerusalem. At the age of 20 he ordered all the pagan altars to be destroyed throughout the whole country. At the age of 28 he noticed that the Temple of God was in bad repair and so he ordered it to be put right. While they did this, someone found a copy of the Law of Moses in an old, dusty cupboard. They realized that they hadn't been studying it or reading it for years. When Josiah read it, he was horrified. He realized why God was warning them. So at the age of 28 he ordered the Law to be read again and carried out throughout the nation.

So the signs up to this point were good. But Josiah didn't realize that you can't make people good by an Act of Parliament. Many people today think that if only our government would pass good laws, then people would behave in a Christian way. But righteousness can't be imposed from above – it must be expressed from within, as God works in the human heart.

Josiah's life ended following an ill-advised attack on the Egyptian army, who were passing through the Holy Land to attack Assyria. He was killed in the ensuing battle, despite being in disguise.

So despite having some influence, Zephaniah failed to turn the nation around. The people didn't listen. But his work was not wasted. There was a young man the same age as Josiah whom God told to pick up the prophetic burden. Jeremiah was charged with telling the people that the reform wasn't working and they needed to return to God.

Making use of Zephaniah

The key application for the believer today concerns judgement.

(a) The Day of Judgement for the whole world will come after death. Judah's condemnation is a foretaste and foreshadowing of what will happen to the world. Jesus twice alludes to Zephaniah in connection with the Second Coming (see Matthew 13:34 and Zephaniah 1:3; Matthew 24:29 and Zephaniah 1:15). So most people will face God's wrath after Jesus returns.

(b) The Day of Judgement for God's people will come before it does for other people. 1 Peter 4:17 reads: 'For it is time for judgment to begin with the family of God; and if it begins with us, what will the outcome be for those who do not obey the gospel of God?'

Zephaniah is a powerful reminder for Christians that they should expect God's discipline, but not lose heart. Discipline in this life is a sign of God's care and assures us that we won't be judged along with the world.

Zephaniah and Revelation

In closing, we must also note the remarkable correlation between the prophet Zephaniah and the outline of the Book of Revelation.

Both Zephaniah and Revelation start with judgement on God's people – Israel and the Church respectively. They both move on to judgements on the nations (see Zephaniah 2; Revelation 4–15). Finally, they move on to the Day of Judgement (Zephaniah 3:1–8; Revelation 20).

But the last word is the final bliss of God's giving a place to his people where they can live for ever (Zephanaiah 3:9–20; Revelation 21–22). In Zephaniah the location is the old Jerusalem, but in Revelation it is the new Jerusalem. In Zephaniah God comes as King, but in Revelation Jesus comes again as King.

In all there are over 400 allusions to the Old Testament in the Book of Revelation, but the closest connection is with the prophet Zephaniah. So it is likely that the apostle John was influenced more by this prophet from centuries before than any other. So a seemingly obscure Old Testament book is actually a central book for our understanding of the future.

PART VIII

HABAKKUK

Introduction

The prophecy of Habakkuk is unusual among the prophetic books. Firstly, in most prophecies God addresses the people through the prophet, but in Habakkuk the prophet addresses God directly, the people not being directly involved at all as the conversation takes place. There are elements of this in other prophecies, notably Jonah and Jeremiah, but no other prophetic book starts in this striking way.

Secondly, in chapter 2 the prophet is instructed to write his message in large letters on a wall.

Then thirdly, chapter 3 is a prophecy set to music, which was fairly rare. It was the earlier leaders such as Moses, Deborah, Samuel, Saul, Elisha and David who had found music to be an inspiration for the prophetic word, although later Ezekiel too made use of music.

We know very little about Habakkuk. We know that he prophesied 20 years after Zephaniah, around 600 BC, and that his name literally means 'someone who embraces'. It was a wrestling term put into colloquial language. We might call him 'Clinger' – not an especially flattering name!

But though his name is not especially pleasant, it accurately describes his relationship with God as it unfolds in the book.

Habakkuk was a man who clung to God, who dared to argue with God, and who insisted on getting answers from God, even if he didn't like the answers when they came. So although we don't know much about the prophet's background, we learn something of his mind, heart and will through his conversations with God recorded in the book. We also gain insights into the key dimensions of his prophetic ministry – his praying (ch. 1), his preaching (ch. 2) and his praising (ch. 3).

The book has great relevance to us today, for it deals with some very basic questions that all thinking believers ask. If God is good and all powerful, why do the innocent suffer and the guilty go free? Why doesn't God do something about the mess that the world is in? Most wrestle with these issues by themselves or with other people. But the best way of dealing with such big questions is to wrestle with God and cling to him until he gives you an answer. Habakkuk gives us a wonderful example of a man who did just that. His boldness and sheer honesty come through in the prophecy, and the book is both challenging and delightful as a result.

In contrast to Zephaniah, Habakkuk is full of 'quotable quotes'. For example, 'Your eyes are too pure to look on evil' (1:13) is a popular verse, though, as we shall see later, we must be careful how we interpret it. Here are some other well-known verses:

> For the earth will be filled with the knowledge of the glory of the Lord, as the waters cover the sea. **(2:14)**

> The Lord is in his holy temple; let all the earth be silent before him. **(2:20)**

> In wrath remember mercy. **(3:2)**

Though the fig-tree does not bud and there are no grapes on
the vines ... yet I will rejoice in the Lord, I will be joyful in
God my Saviour.   **(3:17–18)**

The most famous verse from Habakkuk, which has become the
'Magna Carta' of Protestantism, is 'The just shall live by faith'
(2:4). Martin Luther made this one verse ring around northern
Europe at the time of the Reformation, though, as we shall see
later, it wasn't properly understood.

An outline of the Book of Habakkuk

The prophet (1:1)

Complaining prayer (1:2–2:20)
Complaint: God does too little
Question: Why don't the bad suffer?
Answer: The bad will suffer (the Babylonians)
Complaint: God does too much
Questions: Why use the bad to punish the bad?
Why do the good suffer?
Answers: The good will survive!
The bad will suffer!

Composed praise (3:1–19)
He trembles at God's past action (3:1-16)
He trusts in God's future protection (3:17–19)

The Book of Habakkuk divides clearly into two parts. Chapters
1 and 2 form the first part and chapter 3 is the second part.
The contrast between the first and second parts is enormous,
as we can see in the table below:

Chapters 1–2	Chapter 3
Wrestling with God	Resting in God
Miserable	Happy
Shouting	Singing
Prayer	Praise
Impatient	Patient
Asks for justice	Asks for mercy
Down in the dumps	On a high
God is inactive (in the present)	God is active (in the past and future)

The table demonstrates the enormous change between the first and second parts, leading to the inevitable question: What has happened to Habakkuk for this contrast to be so apparent? We will need to go into the prophecy in detail to find out what has changed him.

Complaining prayer (1:2–2:20)

God does too little (1:2–11)

Habakkuk told God exactly what he was thinking. At first he complained that God was doing too little and then he complained that God was doing too much – God couldn't win!

He believed in interrogatory prayer. Intercessory prayer is when you ask God for things, but interrogatory prayer is when you ask God questions. It is a very important type of prayer, which I find most helpful. I simply ask God a question, and if something comes into my mind – especially if it is something very unexpected – I accept it as from God. Nine times out of ten it proves to be so.

For example, when our daughter died, we were astonished to find out how much she had been doing for the Lord. She never talked about it, but she had been in regular touch with missionaries in China, Africa and Haiti, to name just a few. Furthermore, she was a worship leader in the church, and was so loved that the whole church mourned her. When I was talking to the Lord about her I said, 'Lord, I am very proud of our daughter, but how do you feel about her? What is your opinion?' Immediately the words came to me: 'She is one of my successes.' So at her funeral I preached on the theme, 'Are you one of the Lord's successes or one of his failures?' If you have never heard from the Lord in your life, then try asking this question: 'Lord, is there anything in my life that you don't like?' If you really want to hear from God, just ask him that question.

The social setting of Habakkuk helps us to understand his questions. There had been no word from God in the 20 years since the time of Zephaniah. The nation had continued its downward slide, in defiance of Zephaniah's message. King Josiah had not achieved what he had hoped for with his reforms and met a premature death at Megiddo in 608 BC. Habakkuk prophesied during the time of his successor, Jehoiakim, who became a very worldly, selfish king. His palace was extended but the poor became poorer under his reign. Bribery, corruption, lawlessness and oppression filled the streets of Jerusalem. It became so dire that it wasn't safe to walk the streets at night alone. The Assyrians, who had taken away the 10 tribes, were now in decline, so there was no strong world power as such.

Why don't the bad suffer?

This feeling that nothing was happening while Jerusalem deteriorated was at the heart of Habakkuk's concern. When he addressed God he built his case very carefully. He knew that God's nature must be reflected in his attitude and actions and that he wouldn't wipe his people out, but he also knew that God must execute punishment and ordain judgement on sin. So he complained to God that he was doing nothing about the violence and corruption in his holy city. He wanted God to reverse the trends, to change society and to restore law and order.

God does too much (1:12–2:20)

God was gracious in responding to Habakkuk's anger, but Habakkuk was surprised and dismayed by the five responses that God gave:

1 Open your eyes a bit wider – watch.
2 You are in for a very big surprise.
3 I have planned something that will happen in your lifetime.
4 I haven't told you what I am doing because you wouldn't believe it.
5 I have already begun to do something and you have missed it.

In short, God tells Habakkuk that he has noticed the evil in Jerusalem and has already acted by raising up the Babylonians to punish the people of Judah. At this time Babylon was just a growing city on the Tigris River. Few had heard of it, and it had barely been mentioned in the Bible up to this point. But when two messengers from Babylon visited King Hezekiah and were shown around his palace, Isaiah realized the danger and predicted that one day Babylon would take away everything from the palace and Temple that the king had shown the two men.

At the time Babylon was too small for the prophecy to have seemed likely, but in Habbakkuk's day this prophecy was nearing fulfilment, and Habakkuk was understandably shocked.

It was just as if God had said he was going to bring Nazi Germany to punish England. But we can see throughout history that this is how God typically deals with nations. He raises up one nation to deal with another. So such activity need not surprise us.

THEY ARE WORSE THAN WE ARE

But Habakkuk is surprised and dismayed. He now complains that God is doing 'too much', for he knows that the Babylonians have a worse reputation than the Assyrians, who had eventually overpowered Israel (the 10 tribes) and taken them to an exile from which they never returned. But the Babylonians would be even worse. They were the first nation to introduce a scorched-earth policy whereby they removed every trace of life from the land of the peoples they conquered. Habakkuk realized that if the Babylonians came to Jerusalem there would be nothing left. This explains the meaning of the well-known words at the end of the book: 'Though the fig tree does not blossom, and there are no grapes on the vine, and there are no sheep or cattle in the pen …' This is how the land would be after the visit of the Babylonian army.

THEY WILL NOT DISCRIMININATE BETWEEN GOOD AND BAD

Habakkuk also reminds God that there are some righteous people in the city of Jerusalem who would die along with the wicked. Although he doesn't say so directly, the implication is that he is among them. He is angry that God is using people who are more wicked than Judah to execute the punishment. In Habakkuk's reasoning this is immoral, so he utters the much-quoted words, 'Your eyes are too pure to look on evil' (1:13). Habakkuk was trying to suggest that God's very character was impugned by what he had promised to do. But in so doing he says something about God that isn't true. God is pure and holy, but that does not mean that he cannot look on evil, for he has to watch evil being committed every day. He watches every rape, every mugging, every act of cruelty. Habakkuk has his own view of what God will or won't look upon, but he is wrong.

When Habakkuk has finished arguing with God, he goes up to the watchtower in Jerusalem and sits on the wall. He says he is going to watch to see if God will really do what he has said. He is almost saying, 'I am going to call your bluff. I dare you to bring them, Lord.'

WRONG PLACE

In reply God tells Habakkuk that he is achieving nothing by sitting on the watchtower. He should go down into the street and write what God has told him on the wall so that passers-by can read it – the first advertising hoarding in the Bible! Habakkuk should be warning the people, not sitting at a distance to see whether God will do what he has promised.

When God reveals to us what he is going to do, he does it so that we can tell people to get ready, not so that we can wait around to see if he does it.

WRONG TIME

God also tells Habakkuk that if he stays in a tower he won't see anything for quite a time. He might jump to the wrong conclusion about what God is doing. God says, 'The revelation awaits an appointed time.' So he needs to take a long-term view and warn the people of what will come.

The good will survive

It is during this interchange that God tells Habakkuk that 'the just will live by faith' (2:4b), which became the most famous verse in the book, because of its use by Luther during the time of the Reformation. But as we hinted earlier, although much good was accomplished through the Reformation, the verse itself was misunderstood.

If we look at the verse in context, Habakkuk is saying that the Babylonians will kill the righteous as well as the wicked. God is saying in the verse that he will protect the righteous (or 'the just') – they will survive, provided that they remain faithful to him. When the Babylonians arrive there will be many who will lose faith in God, believing that he has let them down. But God says that those who go on believing in him will survive that coming judgement.

So this is the real meaning of the verse. The word 'faith', both in the Hebrew and in the Greek languages, includes the idea of faithfulness. It is faithfulness that saves; they must *go on* believing and *keep* faith.

This intrepretation fits in with the way that faith is some-times used as a noun in the Old Testament. It is used about faithfulness in marriage. Faith in marriage is to stay together till death parts the couple. It is also used of Moses when he kept his arms outstreched while the children of Israel won the battle against the Amalekites. He was faithful in standing for the people.

The principle is the same in the New Testament. Believing in Jesus on one occasion isn't faith. True faith is continuing to believe in him, whatever happens. This is why we read in the Gospels, 'He who endures to the end shall be saved.'

The rest of the New Testament also uses the verse in this way. Three different passages quote Habakkuk 2:4 and interpret 'the just will live by faith' as referring to people *continuing* to believe.

In Romans 1:16–17 Paul writes: 'I am not ashamed of the gospel, because it is the power of God for the salvation of everyone who believes: first for the Jew, then for the Gentile. For in the gospel a righteousness from God is revealed, a righteousness that is by faith from first to last, just as it is written: "The righteous will live by faith."' In other words, it begins with faith and it ends with faith. Salvation is enjoyed by *going on* believing.

In Galatians 3:11 Paul contrasts faith with the self-righteous keeping of the law. He says that no one is justified by the law, and quotes Habakkuk 2:4 as the reason, because 'The righteous will live by faith.' Living by faith is not a single act but a continuing attitude for a whole lifetime. Only *ongoing trust* in Christ saves.

The writer of Hebrews also uses the verse to back an argument about the need for *ongoing trust*. In 10:39, having quoted Habakkuk 2:4, he adds, 'But we are not of those who shrink back and are destroyed, but of those who believe [i.e. go on believing] and are saved.'

So it is clear that these passages underline a most important correction to the way in which the text was used during the Reformation and since. The verse must not be interpreted as saying that if a person has believed for just one minute – that is, if they have made a 'commitment to Christ' – their life is safe. This is a gross misuse of the text. The just shall live by 'keeping faith' with the Lord. There is complacency amongst some Christians, who use an unscriptural phrase – 'Once saved, always saved' – as if a moment or short period of trusting will ensure that they escape God's wrath. But it is those who keep faith with the Lord who survive the worst that happens.

The bad will suffer

But having used the Babylonians to judge, God does not let them get away with their evil. In the second half of chapter 2 there is a series of woes addressed to Babylon. The word 'woe' in Scripture is a curse and should never be used by a Christian unless they are sure what they are doing. When Jesus said 'woe', awful things happened, and he said 'woe' as often as he said 'blessed'. For example, there were 250,000 people living on the shores of Galilee in Jesus' day in four major towns. Jesus pronouced a curse on three of the towns. He said, 'Woe to you, Capernaum', 'Woe to you, Bethsaida', 'Woe to you, Korazin', but he didn't say 'Woe' to Tiberias. If you go to Galilee today you will have to stay in Tiberias, for it is the only town there is. The towns that Jesus said 'Woe' to have all disappeared.

Habakkuk lists five reasons why the Babylonians will incur God's wrath:

1 **Injustice** They plundered the nations that they overran, with little regard for their people.
2 **Imperialism** They dictated how the nations that they conquered should live, with little concern for justice and little pity for the people's plight.
3 **Inhumanity** God condemned their bloodshed, their use of slave labour to build Babylon, and their callous treatment of their enemies. They even took babies by the legs and bashed their heads against rocks.
4 **Intemperance** They were an ill-disciplined people when it came to alcohol, and did terrible things when they were drunk. This included the destruction of animals and even trees. When Israel went to war God forbade them to cut down a single tree unless they needed it for the war.
5 **Idolatry** They worshipped lifeless wood, stone and metal idols, ignoring the true God of Judah. At this stage, of course, Babylon had not reached the height of her powers, but even so Habakkuk was instructed to announce the doom.

So the rebuke is for actions that violate the conscience. At no point are the Babylonians judged for failure to keep God's Law. They don't have a covenant with God. But they are judged for doing things that they know in their hearts are wrong. God's judgement of them is a reminder to the people of God that he is concerned about their behaviour in these areas too.

So God answers Habakkuk's argument by saying that the good will survive and the bad will suffer. God is not blind to what has been going on, nor is he impotent, nor is he unjust. He is the living God, in contrast to the dead, lifeless idols fashioned by men.

Having given Habakkuk the answer he sought, God then adds, 'Let all the earth be silent.' God is effectively saying, 'You have your answer. Now shut up!'

Composed praise (3:1–19)

It was while he was quiet that Habakkuk saw the light. He stopped arguing with God and thought about what God had said, and his whole mood changed. He understood that God had a much greater picture than he did, and also a longer-term view. Although he couldn't see God at work now, God would act when the time was right.

The last chapter is set to music, composed in his own mind with his own hand, reflecting this change of heart. The musical instructions as to how the singing should be accompanied – 'with stringed instruments' – are included at the end of the chapter. So when we come to chapter 3 we have a completely different outlook expressed. Indeed, the text is so different here that scholars claim that chapter 3 was an addition.

He trembles at God's past action (3:1–16)

In chapter 3 Habakkuk changes his focus on three occasions. He starts with 'he', moves on to 'you', then finishes with 'I', as if he gets more personally involved as the chapter progresses.

HE (3:2–7)

Habakkuk now focuses on God's power in the period covering the exodus, the wilderness and the conquest of Canaan. He asks God to do it again. What he has heard about, he wants to see. This time there is no request for a change of plan, no questioning of God's activities. He only asks that in his wrath, God might remember to be merciful.

So if chapter 1 focused on Israel's violence and chapter 2 on the Babylonians' violence, chapter 3 calls for God's violence.

YOU... (3:8–15)

In these verses Habakkuk is involved in the vision. He is still asking questions, but this time they are right ones. He reflects on God's majesty and power in creation. He knows that God has the power to do whatever he pleases. He is now content to 'wait patiently for the day of calamity'.

He trusts in God's future protection (3:17–19)

I (3:16–19)

The change from 'you' to 'I' gives an important insight as Habakkuk reflects on his own reaction to the news of the Babylonian invasion. He is 'walking by faith', even if there is no visible evidence of God's word coming true. He speaks of the pressures from inside – how his emotions are artificially lifted by his vision of the future. But at the same time he faces pressures from the outside that are depressing him. He doesn't look forward to the disaster that is about to come on the people, but nevertheless he is able to 'rejoice in the Lord'. In chapter 1 his argument came from a mind that was concentrated on the present. But now he looks back into the past and sees that God has always intervened. He looks into the future and sees that God will intervene again, and so he is prepared to wait. In our age we focus so much on the present that we have little or no time for the past or the future. But it is this perspective that will help us when injustice overwhelms us.

I have put chapter 3 into verse, to the tune of Beethoven's 'Ode to Joy'. It seems a fitting way to end our study.

Lord, your fame has gone before you from the time your
    arm was bared,
Tales of deeds so overwhelming, even listening makes me
    scared.
Now today, O Lord, repeat them, prove that you are still the
    same –
But in wrath remember mercy for the honour of your name.

Look, this Holy God descending spreads the sky with
    glorious rays,
Trailing from his hand of power, earth is filled with sounds
    of praise;
But the guilty nations tremble, plague and pestilence their
    fears:
Even ancient mountains crumble when the infinite appears.

Are you angry with the rivers? Is your wrath upon the
    streams?
Do you rage against the ocean with your horse and chariot
    teams?
Writhing hills and flooded valleys, sun and moon stand still
    in fear
At the glint of flying arrows, lightning of your flashing spear.

Striding through the earth in vengeance, threshing nations
    till it's done,
All to save your chosen people, rescue your anointed one.
You have crushed their wicked leader, stripped him bare and
    split his head;
So his storming, gloating warriors scatter to the wind
    instead.

Having heard the final outcome, knowing all and not just
    part,
Great emotion grips my body, quivering lips and pounding
    heart,
Trembling legs give way beneath me, yet with patience will
    I wait,
When the foe invades my country, certain of his dreadful
    fate.

Though the fig tree does not blossom and the vine is void
    of grapes,
Though the olive trees are barren and the fields produce
    no crops,
Though no lambs are in the sheepfold and no cattle in the
    stall –
Yet will I enjoy my saviour, glad that God is all in all.

Joyfully I face the future with my failing strength restored
And my angry questions answered by this marvellous
    sovereign Lord.
See my heart and feet are leaping like a deer upon the
    heights –
Set my words to holy music, voices and stringed
    instruments.

PART IX

JEREMIAH AND
LAMENTATIONS

Introduction

Jeremiah is a key figure in the Old Testament and is one of the best known of all the prophets. But his book is not one of the most popular. Here are three reasons why people don't like it. It is daunting, difficult and depressing.

Daunting

It is 52 chapters long, second only to Isaiah's 66 chapters. Legend says that Jeremiah visited Southern Ireland and kissed the Blarney Stone and received the gift of the gab! The length reflects both the number of prophecies in his 40-year career and the dedication of his secretary in writing them down. But for many readers it is too long a book to tackle with any enthusiasm.

Difficult

The book is in neither chronological nor topical order and so it is hard to follow. The writings have been bunched together in what seems to be an arbitrary fashion. We might call it a collection of collections. This is compounded by the fact that Jeremiah seems to change his viewpoint. Critics take particular delight in finding contradictions in his preaching. He is totally against Babylon in the early years, but then later advised people to submit to Babylon. It is one of the reasons why he was called a political traitor. The truth is that over 40 years his message changed according to the circumstances and the course that God had intended him to follow.

Depressing

The most popular reason for disliking Jeremiah is that it is one of the most depressing parts of the Bible. There seems to be nothing but bad news for Judah, with Jeremiah sharing the pain he felt at what was happening to the nation and in his own ministry. The very name 'Jeremiah' in the English language has come to mean being a wet blanket. In literature a 'jeremiad' is a mournful poem or dirge. So Jeremiah has got a bad press. Once again, this is not the whole picture. There is good news in his prophecy, but it is hidden among so much bad news that it is easily overlooked.

But in spite of these difficulties, it is a wonderful book. Of all the characters in the Bible, I identify most with Jeremiah. I once preached my way through the whole book and had to stop twice because I was getting so emotionally involved. It was almost too much to share it. It was as a result of that series of sermons that the prophecy came that I was to leave that church and travel, and so the book means a lot to me personally.

It is fascinating because there is a lot of human interest in the book, which draws the reader into understanding Jeremiah and empathizing with his situation. The prophet reveals his heart and his inner struggles more than any other prophet. But there is also a divine interest because it is packed with information about God. If you study Jeremiah seriously you will understand God much better.

The moment

Jeremiah began preaching in the seventh century BC, almost at the end of the life of the two tribes in the south, who went into exile in 586 BC (though some were deported even earlier). He lived during the reigns of seven different kings of Judah: Manasseh, Amon, Josiah, Jehoahaz, Jehoiakim, Jehoiachin and Zedekiah. His 40-year prophetic career was during the reigns of the last five.

He spoke at a traumatic time for the people of God. The 10 tribes in the north had been taken into exile by Assyria, leaving the two tribes of God's people living in and around Jerusalem. Isaiah and Micah had now gone, their messages largely unheeded. Jeremiah is the last prophet to speak to the people and warn them that it was almost too late to stop the disaster from coming.

His birth was in the reign of Manasseh, the evil king who had sawn the prophet Isaiah in half inside a hollow tree for prophesying against him. If this evil wasn't bad enough, he also sacrificed his own babies to the devil and filled Jerusalem's streets with the blood of innocent people. Two boys of significance were born in his reign – Josiah, who became king, and Jeremiah. Manasseh was replaced by another wicked king, Amon, who lasted a few years before Josiah found himself on the throne at the tender age of eight. It was during his reign that the Book of Deuteronomy was found in a dusty old cupboard in the Temple. Josiah was horrified to read that the curses of God were on the land and the people. So he tried to reform the people but failed.

It is interesting that although Jeremiah was one of Josiah's contemporaries, he was silent about the reforms. Jeremiah doesn't mention Josiah and the Books of Kings don't mention Jeremiah. It is almost as if Jeremiah realized that a reform ordered by the king did not change people's hearts. While it looked good, outwardly the situation hadn't changed. Josiah's ill-advised battle with the Egyptians, in which he was killed at Megiddo, proved in part that problems still remained.

Josiah's death lead to a succession of evil, weak kings. It was during the reigns of the last four of these bad kings that Jeremiah did the bulk of his work, which is one reason why he is seen as being so negative. At times he expresses the hopeless feeling of 'It's too late!' but also has this tiny hope that if they repent, God will yet change the situation.

This tension came from an illustration that Jeremiah was given by God. In chapter 18 God tells him to visit the potter's house and observe the potter as he makes vessels, depending upon the clay at his disposal. Many assume that the message concerns God's ability to choose to do whatever he wants with us. Choruses have been written to this effect with lines such as 'You are the potter, I am the clay'. But this is not the lesson that Jeremiah picked up. He saw the potter's intention to make a beautiful vase but, because the clay would not run in his hands, he put it back into a lump, threw it on the wheel again and made a thick, crude pot. God asked Jeremiah if he had learned the lesson. Who decided what the clay would become? The answer is that the clay decided, because it wouldn't run with the potter's original intention. So the message was that God wanted to make the clay into a beautiful shape, but if the clay would not respond, he would make an ugly shape instead. So in the context of Jeremiah's times, God was saying that even at this late stage his people could repent and change and become the beautiful vessel that he had intended. So there is a dynamic relationship between God and people in the Bible. God is not dealing with puppets and decreeing what shall be. Rather, he wants a response from us and will make us what he wants us to be if we cooperate.

But the parable of the potter had a further lesson. The ugly clay pot was baked and became hard so that it couldn't be changed, and then Jeremiah was to take that hard pot, break it and throw the pieces into the valley of Hinnom where the rubbish was thrown. God is saying that if we harden our hearts we will reach the point where we cannot be changed into a beautiful state. So at that point God will break us. God prefers our life to be beautiful, and if we will respond to him he will make it so.

At this time Jeremiah demonstrates that all is not doom and gloom. He tells them that there is a little hope. But eventually the book ends with Zedekiah, the very last king of Judah, who was finally taken away by the Babylonians. He was forced to watch his sons being killed and then had his eyes put out, and was taken away blind. It is a tragic episode in the life of the people of God. It seemed to be an end, but there was still more to come.

The man

Jeremiah is a most unusual name. In Hebrew it can mean either 'to build up' or 'to throw down' – a bit like the English words 'raise' and 'raze', which sound the same but have opposite meanings – 'to make higher' or 'to destroy completely'. The name perfectly described his ministry. His basic message for 40 years was that God pulls down those who disobey and builds up those who obey.

He was born at Anathoth (modern Anatah), three miles north-east of Jerusalem looking down on the Dead Sea. He was appointed a prophet by God before he was born. Like John the Baptist, he was set aside while he was still in his mother's womb. He became a very diffident, sensitive, shy youth.

He was born into a priestly family but the family line was under
God's judgement. A curse had been placed on the house of Eli –
none of his descendants would see old age because of his sins.
Therefore God had to get this man started early if he was going
to get 40 years out of him! A lover of nature, he often used
nature to illustrate God's messages, particularly birds.

He was probably about 17 when he began to preach and he
was very, very nervous. God reassured him that he would make
his forehead like brass, so none of the hostile looks or com-
ments of the people would intimidate him. Anyone who has
spoken in public will know what that means.

His life as a prophet was exceedingly tough. He had to
move to Jerusalem, three miles away, because his family were
going to assassinate him. His 40-year career ran alongside
Habakkuk, Zephaniah, Ezekiel and Daniel, and he was in the
thick of the political world. He advised his people to surrender
to the Babylonians, and the people hated him. No one likes
a policy of appeasement. The Babylonians gave Jeremiah the
choice of going to Babylon with his people or staying in Judah
– which was really no choice, for he didn't like the Babylonians
and his people didn't like him.

In the end he finished up in Egypt. Some Jews kidnapped
him and took him a long way up the River Nile to the
Elephantine Island, where the Ark of the Covenant had already
been taken. (It is probably now in Ethiopia.) This is where he
died, alone. It is a sad story.

The method

Speaking

Although he was a speaker, most of his speaking was in poetry
– distinguished in many Bibles by shorter lines, as opposed to

prose, which looks more like a newspaper column. As a rule, when God speaks in prose he is communicating his thoughts from his mind to the mind of the reader, but when God speaks in poetry he is communicating his heart to the reader's heart. Poetry is, of course, heart language, and most of Jeremiah's prophecy is in poetry. Unfortunately, too many people treat the Bible purely as a source of understanding God's thoughts and fail to notice that it is a very emotional book. I believe the finest translation from Hebrew into English, which communicates the emotions of the Hebrew language, is the Living Bible. It is the most accurate translation of God's feelings, though not the most accurate translation of his thoughts.

Acting

Sometimes Jeremiah's message was delivered through drama in order to provoke comment. On one occasion he buried some dirty old underwear. When asked why, he replied that the underwear depicted the inner lives of the people. We have already noted the important lesson gained from observing the potter. Another time he wore a cattle yoke as a burden to demonstrate the need to submit to the Babylonians. When everyone in Jerusalem was trying to sell their property because they knew that when the Babylonians came it would be worthless, God told Jeremiah to buy property. He bought a field from his relative who was desperately anxious to sell. Jeremiah knew that one day the people would return from Babylon, and this investment enabled him to 'put his money where his mouth was'.

Other dramatic illustrations included hiding stones, throwing books into the river Euphrates and carrying a jar on his head round the city like a woman. They seem bizarre, but they got the message across.

Writing

Jeremiah's prophecies were preserved by Baruch, one of God's 'backroom boys', who was like a secretary to Jeremiah. At one point the prophecies enraged King Jehoiakim so much that he cut them up with a knife and burned them. After 23 years of ministry, Jeremiah was not allowed to speak publicly, so it was Baruch who ensured that his voice was still heard. Here was a man who would never, in one sense, do great things himself, but who made it possible for others to hear the word of God. In fact, God rewards those who work in secret more than those who work publicly. Without that work, his words would have been lost.

The message

We have noted that the Book of Jeremiah is not in chronological or topical order and so it can be difficult to read, but there is a general pattern that will aid comprehension:

Prologue – Jeremiah's personal call (1:1–19)

The sinning nation (2–45)
627–605 BC Immediate retribution (2–20)
(mostly poetry)
Babylon destroys Assyria (612 BC)
Babylon defeats Egypt (605 BC)
605–585 BC: Ultimate restoration (21–45)
(mostly prose)
Babylon deports Judah

The surrounding nations (46–51)

Epilogue – national catastrophe (52)

The prologue in chapter 1 is about how Jeremiah was called by God as a young man, and how he was terribly shy and afraid of public speaking.

Chapters 2–45, 'The sinning nation', includes Jeremiah's prediction that Judah's punishment is coming very quickly. It covers the years 627–605 BC. It is mainly poetry, which means that Jeremiah is communicating God's feelings to them – in particular his regret and his anger. God has a conflict of emotions. He loves them but he cannot let them go on as they are. The prediction that Babylon will destroy Assyria and defeat Egypt comes here. The kings of Judah had mistakenly assumed that if they made a treaty with Egypt they would be protected.

Chapters 21–45 contain good news as Jeremiah looks beyond the despair of exile to the ultimate restoration. After he knew that the situation was hopeless, he gave them a longer-term view of the ultimate restoration of the people. This section is mainly prose, for it conveys mainly thoughts rather than feelings from God. In the long term, after Babylon has deported Judah and Jerusalem is devastated, some of the people will come back and rebuild Jerusalem, so the situation is not totally lost.

Chapters 46–51 cover God's judgement on the nations that surround Judah. The restoration will be accompanied by the judgement on those who have caused her troubles. That's how the God of justice operates in history.

Chapter 52 is a kind of epilogue about the dreadful national catastrophe that was breaking on Jeremiah's people. It describes how Jeremiah was taken away to Egypt, and Jerusalem was left empty and devastated. It is not a happy ending.

Like the other prophets

A lot of Jeremiah's message is the same as that of the other prophets. In fact, if you read through the prophets one after the other, you could easily get bored. For it is the same old story of idolatry, immorality and injustice. The prophets were observing the same decline. Jerusalem was filled with violence so that children couldn't even play in the streets and old people dared not come out.

There are four major thrusts of his message which we find in all the other prophets. Indeed, when Jeremiah was nearly put to death, somebody remembered that Micah had said exactly the same thing years before, and this saved Jeremiah's life.

1. APOSTATE PEOPLE

The people were totally corrupt. Idolatry and immorality were the two main problems. Some of the awful practices of the surrounding nations were being practised by the people of God, including child sacrifice in the Valley of Hinnom and idols being brought into the Temple of God, in direct contravention of the second commandment. There was also moral rottenness and broken marriages.

God calls Jeremiah to preach that certain people were responsible for the situation.

The prophets

Jeremiah's ministry was bedevilled by people around him who claimed that they were prophets too but gave the opposite message to Jeremiah. In chapter 23 he attacks these false prophets, accusing them of never having stood in the counsel of God and listened to what God was telling them. Instead they copied their messages from each other or invented them from their own minds, telling people what they wanted to hear.

In particular they were saying, 'Peace, peace' when there was
no peace. They claimed there was no need to worry. After all,
Jerusalem was God's city and he would look after the Temple.
But Jeremiah was scathing of those who put their security in
the Temple. He tells them that they have turned it into a den
of thieves, and warns them that they can't assume that just
because they are God's people, they won't be judged.

There is a similar lesson in the New Testament. The
majority of Jesus' warnings about hell were given to born-
again believers! Yet I meet many believers who have no fear of
hell because they assume that it can never happen to those who
call themselves Christians.

But Jesus teaches that we must continue in our faith if we
are to escape the wrath to come. The apostle Paul reminds
born-again believers that all will appear before the judgement
seat of Christ. We are justified by faith, but judged by works.

The priests

Jeremiah blamed the priests for the nation's sin because they
were supporting what we would call today 'inter-faith festivals'.
They were holding pagan religious services in the name of tol-
erance – just as in the UK today there are services that include
non-Christian religious groups, in the misguided belief that we
are all on different roads leading to the same God.

The princes

The princes (or kings) were condemned for their failure to
uphold God's laws. Jeremiah prophesied that Jehoiakim would
die without mourning and would be buried like an ass – and
his death took place just as Jeremiah had promised. Zedekiah,
the last king, was weak and vacillating, a mere puppet of the
politicians.

Jeremiah's images describing this apostate people are full of sexual metaphors, some of them quite obscene. He likened the people, who were going after foreign gods, to a faithless, adulterous wife going after other men. Hosea had been the first prophet to use this metaphor. Jeremiah asked the people to imagine how God felt with an unfaithful wife. Their integrity in other relationships was also poor. Jeremiah claimed that there was 'not one honest person in Jerusalem'.

One of the most dreadful things he said to them was that they were unable to blush. They had no shame. Their apostasy doesn't even trouble them. God had already divorced the 10 tribes – did they want him to divorce the two tribes as well?

2. IMPENDING DISASTER

The second major thrust of his message that is also shared with other prophets is the theme of impending disaster. When God made promises to Israel at the time of Moses, he made two kinds: 'I bless you when you are obedient' and 'I curse you when you are disobedient.' These were reaffirmed in the Sinai covenant. So when God punishes, he is keeping his promise. Most people think of his faithfulness as keeping on doing good things for us, but his faithfulness is seen in punishing as much as in pardoning.

Jeremiah was specific about what would happen. He received a vision of a boiling pot tilting from the north, and told the people that the danger would come from that direction – not from Assyria, which had taken the 10 tribes away, but from Babylon, whose armies would also invade from the north. He warned them that the danger would come soon. He had a vision of an almond branch bursting into blossom – the sign of spring, and it happens so quickly with an almond tree. In the same way, Judah would suddenly see the Babylonians coming.

3. ULTIMATE RESTORATION

But beyond this doom and gloom comes a ray of hope. Some of the most positive prophecies about the future of the people of God are found in Jeremiah. He prophesied a restored nation with a new covenant with God. The old covenant of Moses wasn't working, because the commandments were written outside of people and not inside them. They were written on stone but needed to be written on the heart. So in chapter 31 we have one of the loveliest predictions in the Old Testament. We are told that God will make a new covenant with the house of Israel and the house of Judah, based on the fact that God will write his laws in the people's hearts. They won't need to be taught about God because they will all know him, and God will forgive them and not remember their sins any more.

Many readers in church stop there, but I want to read on. God also says:

> This is what the Lord says, he who appoints the sun to shine by day, who decrees the moon and stars to shine by night, who stirs up the sea so that its waves roar – the Lord Almighty is his name: 'Only if these decrees vanish from my sight,' declares the Lord, 'will the descendants of Israel ever cease to be a nation before me'   **(31:35–36)**

So the Lord says that only if the heavens above can be measured and the foundations of the earth below can be searched out will he reject all the descendants of Israel because of all they have done. God guarantees that he will keep his side of the covenant. There will always be an Israel and there still is. The fact that the name 'Israel' is back on the map today is proof that God keeps his promises.

Here Jeremiah promises the ultimate restoration of his people. He writes of God bringing them home again with rejoicing, singing and dancing, and states that it will be in 70 years. (This figure later encouraged Daniel when he read the prophecy in the exile and realized that the 70 years were nearly up. The figure may seem arbitrary, but it was carefully calculated as the time required for the land to get its rest, since they had missed the one-year-in-seven rest for the land in the previous 500 years [2 Chronicles 36:21].)

Jeremiah also promised Judah a new leader. He gave him the titles 'the good shepherd', 'the righteous branch', 'the messianic prince', 'the shoot from David's tree', 'the fountain of life'. He promised that this man would come and would restore the throne to them, and the Gentiles would share in Judah's blessing.

4. PUNISHED ENEMIES

Although God would allow the Babylonians to take Judah into exile, he would make sure that they were punished for their cruelty. Habakkuk had majored on this in his prophecy. So Babylon would later be conquered by the Persians in fulfilment of this prophecy (which, in turn, led to the return of the Jews through the decree of Cyrus, the Persian king). Other enemies will also be dealt with: Egypt, Philistia, Moab, Ammon, Edom, Damascus (Syria), Kedar, Hazor and Elam. There's a section at the end of Jeremiah's book which predicts what will happen to all the nations who have attacked Israel or have been unkind to them, and it is God who will exact vengeance, not Israel. Only Egypt and Babylon received any positive comment.

Unlike the other prophets

Having looked at the things that Jeremiah says that are in common with the other prophets, we will now look at the three things he says which are quite unique to him.

1. SPIRITUAL

Jeremiah has been called 'the spiritual prophet', because he is the one prophet who says that religious ritual is worse than useless if your heart isn't in it. In fact, his condemnation of hypocrisy in worship has led some to mistakenly assume that Jeremiah thought the whole system of sacrificial offerings to God was a waste of time. Actually, he was saying that the outward ritual of worship was not all that important, for God was really looking for heart motivation. Did the worshipper really engage in spiritual activity? The body may be circumcised, but is the heart also? The priests were falsely encouraging the idea that religious observance was somehow a substitute for godliness. So Jeremiah needed to put a tremendous emphasis on the spiritual aspect of religious life.

At the same time, Jeremiah was preparing the people for the day when they would lose the Temple and not be able to offer sacrifices. In Babylon they would meet in what became known as 'synagogues'. The word 'synagogue' is a Greek word which means 'to come together'. The people of God would assemble for three things: praising God, praying and reading the Scriptures. In fact, this resembled the New Testament Church situation, when the priesthood had been made redundant by Christ's once-for-all sacrifice. The Church has no temple, altars, incense, priests or sacrifices. The New Testament Church simply came together to celebrate communion, to pray, to praise and to read and study the Scriptures. So the early churches were effectively Christian synagogues. The temptation of the Christian Church from the beginning has been to go back to the ritual of the Temple and to have priests, altars, incense and vestments. But it's a reversion to the Old Testament pattern and not what God intended at all.

Jeremiah was one of the men who liberated the Jews from a dependence on ceremony, so that they could survive without it and still meet together in Babylon. He was the only prophet who could foresee that they would have to find a form of religion without the Temple and all its paraphernalia.

2. INDIVIDUAL

The next unique thing in Jeremiah's prophecy is that he predicts that in the new covenant God will deal with individuals. The Sinai covenant was collective rather than individual, with the whole people, not each person. One of the striking features of the new covenant as it comes in the New Testament is the emphasis on each individual. Jesus was constantly talking about individual followers. Jeremiah describes the contrast: 'In those days people will no longer say, "The fathers have eaten sour grapes, and the children's teeth are set on edge." Instead everyone will die for his own sin; whoever eats sour grapes, his own teeth will be set on edge' (Jeremiah 31:29–30).

In the New Testament, the new covenant is an individual covenant with each person separately. So it is impossible to inherit a place in the Kingdom. God deals with everyone as individuals who need to make their own decisions. So in the New Testament individuals were baptized on their personal confession of Christ.

So in the New Testament we read that on the Day of Judgement each person stands alone and is answerable for their own sins, not anyone else's. So this great switch from God dealing with the people to God dealing with the individual is first sounded in Jeremiah and is then picked up by Ezekiel, and the whole New Testament is based on that understanding.

In many respects Jeremiah's life embodies this principle. He was shut out of the Temple, rejected by his local congregation and so had to survive on his own with God.

3. POLITICAL

Jeremiah gives more political advice to the rulers of Israel than any other prophet. When Judah was shrinking in size, it tried to play off one superpower against another. But Jeremiah warned them not to go to Egypt, because Babylon would defeat them too. His political advice was to give in to Babylon, to cooperate, and to seek to get the best possible terms for surrender. He even describes Nebuchadnezzar, the king of Babylon, as God's servant – which would be like someone from the Church in 1939 telling the British Government to negotiate with Adolf Hitler because God had sent him. It sounded like treason to suggest giving in to a tyrant without even trying to defend Jerusalem.

But the kings of Judah turned down his political advice. He was called a traitor. When he advocated surrender to the Babylonians he put a yoke on his shoulders and walked around Jerusalem as a visual aid of what the people should do. When the king of Babylon arrived in Jerusalem he actually offered to put Jeremiah on his honours list (see chapter 39). We can imagine how the other Jews would feel about this. But this was merely the last episode in a long story of maltreatment and misunderstanding.

The maltreatment

Jeremiah had been persecuted from the very beginning of his ministry. Indeed, the first attempts to kill Jeremiah came from his own relatives in his home area, the village of Anathoth. They plotted to assassinate him because it injured their family pride that this teenager was going around upsetting the whole of Jerusalem. God had a little word for him then: 'I'm only training you for worse things.' What a comfort!

From then on, he was branded a traitor. He was rejected by the other prophets because they were false prophets. He was shunned by the priests because he spoke against the priests' job, the Temple and the sacrifices. The kings regarded him as a political traitor and the people hated him, hatching various plots to end his life.

Not only was Jeremiah threatened with death; he was also close to death on a number of occasions. He was beaten and imprisoned by the priest Pashhur and flung into a dimly lit dungeon. On other occasions he was put in the stocks with his hands and feet locked, and he was pilloried with an iron collar. Finally he was put in a cistern (a kind of deep well shaped like a flask, with a narrow neck so that the water didn't evaporate). When empty of water, it would typically have four or five feet of soft mud in the bottom. So Jeremiah was up to his neck in the slime, with just a little daylight coming through a small hole above his head. He had, of course, to remain standing, or he would have drowned in this mud. He was eventually released by a foreigner who took pity on him, lowered a rope into the cistern and pulled him out.

He was often in hiding because of attacks on his life. There were few remaining in Jerusalem who would seek his advice, and finally he was forcibly removed by the Jews who fled to Egypt. It was here that he died. His death is not recorded in Scripture. One tradition suggests that he was stoned to death (see Matthew 21:35). Whatever happened, it is clear that he died in obscurity, little dreaming that he would become famous throughout the world and that we'd be talking about him 2,500 years later.

The misery

Jeremiah is known as 'the weeping prophet'. The Book of Lamentations shows the pain in his heart for his people, for the land lost and for the city of Jerusalem destroyed. But even in the Book of Jeremiah itself his misery comes out, because he wasn't afraid to let us know how he prayed in those situations.

Physical sufferings

We have seen already some of the physical pain that Jeremiah felt at the hands of those who despised his message. He was certainly not afraid to bare his soul and reveal his feelings. Here was a man deeply hurt by what his people said and did to him, especially when regarded as a traitor by his own family. He hated the notoriety that went with the faithful proclamation of God's message, and also found his ministry extremely lonely.

Mental sufferings

His physical sufferings were bad enough, but he also felt trapped by God. The particular pain was that God had given him no choice. God had called him to the prophetic ministry and had somehow trapped him so that he could do nothing else. His prophecy includes his resentment and the mental and emotional suffering that came out of this loneliness and rejection.

One of the worst things was that marriage could not relieve the burden of his loneliness. God forbade him to marry. This way Jeremiah would not have to see his own children starve when the Babylonians came. His own life thus became a powerful message, just as Hosea's marriage to a prostitute and God's command to Ezekiel not to mourn the death of his wife were messages to the people they spoke to.

We have intimated already that the book gives real insight into Jeremiah's pain, and at the same time provides help for those going through trauma.

On one occasion he said, 'I know, O Lord, that a man's life is not his own, and it's not for a man to direct his steps.' A well-known quote is: 'If I decide that I'll never talk about God again, there is a hidden fire burning in my bones. I am weary with forbearance and I cannot contain it.' The poor man is effectively saying, 'I'm never going to preach another sermon.' And then he says, 'But I can't stop. It's burning in my bones. I've got to let it out.'

He had no choice about preaching, because his heart was burning for God. Even when he made a decision never to preach again, he just found himself out on the streets preaching. In fact, God hadn't really forced him into it – God never forces people. But we can understand his feelings about being trapped.

Jeremiah knew that the people would never listen, and at various points he concludes that he is involved in a hopeless task. God even forbids him to pray for the people (7:16).

Despite this, however, the prayers of Jeremiah are a significant part of the prophecy and include some of the most moving passages (e.g. 1:6; 4:10; 10:23–25; 11:20; 12:1–6; 15:15–18; 17:14–18; 18:19–23; 20:7–18). These nine prayers of Jeremiah are among the most honest of any in Scripture. He tells God exactly how he feels, and as such provides a good example for our prayers.

Lamentations

The Book of Lamentations was written by the prophet Jeremiah, so it is appropriate that we should consider it alongside the Book of Jeremiah. It is one of the saddest books in the whole Bible. Many would compare it with the Book of Job, but Job is sad because of a personal tragedy, whereas in Lamentations Jeremiah is weeping over a national catastrophe. As you read Lamentations you can almost see the tears dropping onto the page and making the ink run. Here's a man weeping his heart out.

In the Greek translation of the Old Testament this book is simply called 'Tears'. In the Hebrew translation it's called 'How', because that was the first word that was read when the scroll of the book was opened. The English title, 'Lamentations', comes from the Latin word for tears.

It was written as Jeremiah saw the desolated city of Jerusalem. He knew too the pain of his people – prior to the destruction of the Temple and the city the people had been under a terrible siege. Mothers were eating their own babies and even eating the afterbirth of women in labour. They were desperate. The whole thing is so, so sad, and so he weeps. It must have been like Hiroshima following the atom bomb, or war-torn Kosovo in recent years.

The fact that the book is written as a series of laments need not surprise us. We know that Jeremiah was a poet, because most of his prophecies were in poetic form. We also know that he was musical and wrote songs, again because of what we find in his book. This highlights the astonishing relationship between prophecy and music. The spirit of prophecy inspires both poetry and music, and vice versa. A number of Old Testament saints who were blessed with the gift of prophecy would ask for music to be played to them before prophesying. Zechariah, Ezekiel and, of course, David were prime examples.

These are not the only laments composed by Jeremiah. He also composed a lament (mentioned in Chronicles) for the boy

king Josiah, who mistakenly thought he could defeat the
Egyptians and was killed at Megiddo. Just as David lamented
over Saul and Jonathan when they were killed in battle against
the Philistines, so Jeremiah composed a lament for the whole
nation to sing when King Josiah died and the promise of his
reign was brought to an untimely end.

Structure

In spite of the passion that Jeremiah feels for the ruined city
and the exiled people, he has composed the lament using strict
guidelines. For once the chapter divisions are in the right
place, with each chapter comprising one of the five songs that
are beautifully and carefully put together.

The device he uses is an acrostic whereby the letters of
the alphabet are a framework for the song or poem. Since the
Hebrew alphabet has 22 letters, each section has 22 verses.

Four of the laments work on this pattern. The third lament
is slightly different, comprising 66 verses, but again the acrostic method is used.

The first poem has 22 verses – one for each letter and three
lines to each verse. The second poem starts again with the first
letter of the Hebrew alphabet. Then comes the third poem,
once again with three verses for each letter. The fourth goes
back to 22 verses, with two lines to each verse. The only poem
that doesn't follow the letters of the alphabet is the last one,
though it too has 22 verses.

WHY USE THIS DEVICE?

1 It's easier to remember. Jeremiah was concerned that the
   people who were left in the land and the people who were
   sent to exile would hear his laments and take them to heart.
   An acrostic helps to achieve this.

2 This method helps to express Jeremiah's complete grief – his 'A to Z' of grief. It has symbolic significance. He is telling a story of grief all the way from alpha to omega, from the beginning to the end.

3 But I think the third reason is most telling. I tried a little experiment. I took a piece of paper and I wrote down the 26 letters of the English alphabet and asked if it would help me to pour out the teachings of Lamentations. I found that's exactly what it does. It took me less than two minutes to write out Jeremiah's Lamentations. I don't claim that it is a great piece of writing, but I do think it summarizes the whole book:

Awful is the sight of the ruined city,
Blood flows down the streets.
Catastrophe has come to my people,
Dreadful is their fate.
Every house has been destroyed,
Families are broken for ever.
God promised he would do this –
Holy is his name.
I am worn out with weeping,
Just broken in spirit,
Knowing not why.
Let me die like the others –
My life has no meaning.
Never again will I laugh
Or dance for joy.
Please comfort me, Lord;
Quieten my spirit,
Remind me of your future plans.
Save your people from despair,
Tell them you still love them.

Understand their feelings,
Vent your anger on their destroyers.
We will again
eXalt your name,
Yield to your will,
Zealous for your reputation.

So the alphabet can be a very useful tool for expressing feelings.

Why did he write a lament at all?

Even given that there was wisdom in using a lament, it is not immediately obvious why he would choose to write in such a way, especially given the size of his other work.

I believe it was because he wanted others to weep with him and sing the songs. Maybe he wanted to send them to the people taken away in exile so that they might express their feelings too. It makes eminent sense, for when people go through tragedy it is vital that they express their feelings. If grief is called for, it must be allowed to be expressed. It is cruel to tell the bereaved to be brave and not to cry. The Jews and the Catholics are two of the best groups in this regard, because they have a tradition of wakes, when they actively encourage tears. Throughout the Bible tears are encouraged. Our Western tendency to admire people who don't weep comes from Greek rather than Hebrew thinking. In modern Israel a man can never get to be Prime Minister unless he can weep over the grave of an Israeli soldier. In Hebrew thinking it takes a man to weep – it's not a sign of weakness.

She, he, I, they, we

The next thing we must notice about the poems is that the personal pronoun changes with each chapter.

In the first poem the personal pronoun is 'she', referring to the city and to the people of the city, called 'daughters of Jerusalem'. In the Old Testament cities and their people are seen as feminine – a tradition also followed in English texts.

Then, in the second poem, the personal pronoun is 'he'. It is a poem about the person who has caused the disaster. It's about God.

The third poem is the longest and becomes very personal, for it is about Jeremiah himself. The chapter focuses on 'I, me, my'.

The fourth poem and chapter is almost impersonal by contrast, with a detached description of 'those, they, theirs'.

The fifth returns to 'we, us' as Jeremiah identifies with his people again. God is no longer 'he', but is directly addressed as 'you, yourself'.

When we study the Bible carefully we do well to notice these little words as clues to the meaning. So the five very different themes require very different titles, reflecting the way Jeremiah has chosen to see the situation.

The five poems

1. THE CATASTROPHE – 'SHE'

The first poem looks at the ruined city and her daughters.

It wasn't just that the whole city had been besieged and then destroyed, nor just that the Temple had gone. What really upset Jeremiah was the fact that this was God's city. He knew that sin was the reason, and this pained him even more. It is clear that Jeremiah was an eye-witness to the events he described. He sees the wrecked buildings, the deserted streets after the exile to Babylon. It is easy to imagine him remonstrating with the few people still left: 'Is it nothing to you, all you who pass by? Aren't you touched by such a dreadful sight?' So the description of the empty, desolate city is vivid, demonstrating the anguish Jeremiah felt when viewing the scene.

2. THE CAUSE – 'HE'

The second poem focuses on the fact that the disaster wouldn't have taken place if Judah had surrendered to the Babylonians, as Jeremiah had suggested. It was painful to know that he could have helped them to avoid it all. Jeremiah knew that God had to allow the exile because he had promised that he would deal with them in this way if they were disobedient, but his frustration at the opportunities they had wasted was no less real. This comes out especially in the second poem, where the anger of God is mentioned five times. Jeremiah knew that there comes a time when God's anger boils over. There are two kinds of anger in the Bible: slow anger that simmers, and the quick temper that blazes away and is over with. Both cause problems at a human level. At a divine level, God is both slow and quick in his anger – though, of course, without the selfish element that characterizes human anger.

The whole emphasis in the Bible regarding God's anger is that if we do not watch God carefully and if we fail to see his anger simmering, we probably won't notice it until it boils over. In Romans 1 we are told that God's anger is already simmering. We are given signs to look for, including exchanging natural relationships for unnatural ones. Another sign is anti-social behaviour and the breakdown of family life. Sadly, in the Western world these things are all too common.

3. THE CURE – 'I'

The third poem is the personal one. Jeremiah realized that God could have wiped out all the people in his anger, but instead he had sent them to Babylon. So they were still alive, the people had not been extinguished and the nation was still a nation. Jeremiah believed that it was because of God's mercy that they had not been entirely consumed. He says, 'Your mercies are fresh every morning.'

It is good to have such an attitude, whatever our problems. We can always look to God's mercy. There is a fundamental difference between the way the world lives and the way the people of God should live. The world lives by *merit* – we live in a 'meritocracy'. You get what you work for. But in the Kingdom of Heaven the basis of life is *mercy*. The world demands rights, but Christians know that they have no rights.

4. THE CONSEQUENCES – 'THEY'

Jeremiah moves on to recall the consequences of not repenting. He even goes back to Eden and God's righteous punishment of Adam and Eve. He wants everybody to know that this desolation does have a purpose. The people need to know that God is involved in dealing with sin, but will also be involved in deliverance.

5. THE CRY – 'WE'

The last poem is simply a prayer, a plea for God's mercy. Jeremiah knows that God is their only hope, and so turns his despair into a prayer that God will indeed restore his people once more to the land.

One theme that appears in all five poems is the word 'sin'. Almost every page of the Old Testament has sin on it – sometimes just the word, sometimes sinful deeds. By contrast, there is salvation on almost every page of the New Testament.

Jeremiah acknowledges honestly that the people's sin deserves this judgement, but at the same time he cries out to God for the mercy that will restore them. That's why we call this book 'Lamentations' – plural. It's really five different songs of lament and sorrow.

To this very day the whole of Lamentations is sung once a year in every synagogue on the ninth day of Abib (July), because that is the exact date on which the Babylonians destroyed the Temple.

Every year to this day Jews remember the exodus in the Passover, and the loss of the Temple on the ninth of Abib. Every July you can go to the synagogue and you will hear them mourn. The amazing thing is that the ninth of Abib is not only the day when they lost the First Temple – on that very day in AD 70 Titus came and smashed the Second Temple.

On the exact date when they were lamenting the loss of the First Temple, they lost the Second Temple – and Jesus, of course, predicted that. Just as Jeremiah came to warn them about the loss of the First Temple, Jesus came to warn them about the loss of the Second. This is why Jesus and Jeremiah have been bracketed together so often.

When Jesus said to the disciples, 'Who do men say that I am?' they replied that he had been likened to Jeremiah. This prophet may not seem an obvious choice, but his life was a perfect parallel to Jesus' life. So just as Jeremiah could say, 'A man's foe shall be there of his own household', so Jesus too had problems with his own home area. The people tried to throw Jesus off a cliff in his home town of Nazareth. Indeed, Jesus escaped five assassination attempts in all. Also, some of Jesus' acts were in the same spirit as those of Jeremiah. When Jesus cleansed the Temple and used a whip against the Jews who were turning the Temple into a greedy money-changers' centre, he quoted Jeremiah, 'How dare you make my Father's house into a den of thieves!'

Jesus was a Jeremiah in the popular mind. Jeremiah himself at one stage said, 'I feel like a lamb led to the slaughter.' Jesus, for his part, reminded the people that their ancestors had stoned and rejected the prophets who had been sent to them.

Links with Jesus

On the north side of Jerusalem is a cave which in Jewish tradition is known as 'Jeremiah's Grotto', because they believe that it is where Jeremiah went to pray when he was lonely and hurt and in pain. The grotto is a cave in a hill called Golgotha, where we believe that Jesus died on the cross.

One of the things that Jesus said on his way to Calvary was, 'If they do these things in the green tree, what shall be done in the dry?' He was telling the people of Jerusalem not to weep for him but for themselves, for the days were coming when things would be much worse. He was pointing to AD 70, just 40 years ahead. Forty years was the period of testing. God gave the Jews 40 years to respond to his crucified and risen Son. But as a people they remained hard-hearted, so 40 years later the Temple was pulled down again.

Destinies

There are two destinies held before believers in the New Testament – one is weeping and wailing and gnashing of teeth. Whenever Jesus used these words, he was talking to his own disciples, though many assume they should have been directed at unbelievers. The other possible destiny for us as the people of God is that God will wipe away all tears from our eyes. So in a sense the two destinies facing us both involve tears – either we are weeping for ever or having God wipe away the tears.

Not only that, but the world is facing the same prospect. The book that quotes Jeremiah and Lamentations more than any other is the Book of Revelation, which focuses on the end times. Half of the New Testament quotes from Jeremiah are in Revelation and are applied to the city of Babylon. Babylon in Revelation is the final world finance centre – the city that is going to be destroyed. When Babylon is destroyed the world will weep over it, but according to Revelation, Christians will sing the 'Hallelujah Chorus'. Very few people listening to Handel's *Messiah*, with its magnificent 'Hallelujahs', realize that it's a celebration of the world's stock exchange going bust! The world banks will become bankrupt and the whole financial system that man has built up will collapse.

Revelation 18 finishes with quote after quote from Jeremiah. Lamentations talks about the ruin of Jerusalem. But God will bring a new city down from heaven to earth – the new Jerusalem, like a bride adorned for her husband. This is where believers will live, on a new earth in a new Jerusalem for ever.

PART X

OBADIAH

Introduction

Obadiah was the first of the pre-exilic prophets and his book is the shortest in the Old Testament, at just 21 verses. He spoke in 845 BC, and this opened a period of 300 years during which prophet after prophet after prophet warned the people of God not to continue in their present course of action.

We know that Joel came soon after Obadiah because he quotes him, reminding the people of what God had already said to them. In particular he picked up one phrase that Obadiah introduced – 'the Day of the Lord' – a phrase used in other Old Testament prophecies and in the New Testament. It is the day when God comes to put wrongs right, and we looked at it in detail at the end of Joel.

The Book of Obadiah is included at the end of this volume because its focus is on the events at the very end of the pre-exilic period, when the people of Judah were exiled into Babylon.

Some prophets had two messages – one for God's people, Israel, and one for the nations around Israel. Obadiah spoke to Edom, one of Israel's neighbours, a region to the south-east of the Dead Sea. It is the only prophecy by Obadiah that we possess today, and it may have been the only one he gave.

We know very little about Obadiah except that his name means 'the worshipper or servant of Yahweh'. Most of his message is a prediction about the future which came as a vision. It is a visual rather than a verbal message. The state of Edom was located in what we call trans-Jordan, the territory to the east of the Jordan valley. It was part of the land that had been promised to the people of Israel but had never actually been occupied by them. Under King David, Edom had become a satellite state, in much the same way as Poland and Latvia became satellite states of Russia. As soon as David's empire began to break up, Edom sought its own freedom and rebelled against Israel. They had two cities, Bosrah and Sela (known today as Petra), situated on one of the most important roads of the Middle East, from Europe to Arabia.

Petra is a most unusual place. It includes what looks like a cathedral carved out of red sandstone and hundreds of temples carved out of the rock, all round a huge empty circle in the middle of the mountains. Towering above Petra is Mount Seir, around 2,000 feet high. The prophecy of Obadiah is about that mountain.

The architecture of the temples is superb, and the view from the top of the mountain takes in the Red Sea and the Dead Sea. It provided an impregnable fortress for the Edomites who lived in the caves. But they were a godless people. Archaeologists have found altars where they offered humans alive to their gods.

Obadiah says they were full of pride. They believed that nothing could defeat them – not even God. So it was God himself who did just that, and that is the essence of Obadiah's message.

It is significant that the God of Israel is seen here as the God of other nations. This theme is constant throughout the Bible, but it must have sounded radical in a day when every nation had its god, and today as well when many believe that each person should be left to worship the god they prefer without having to worry anyone else.

But Christians believe there is just one God, who will judge people of every other religion too. The God of Israel is the God with whom every nation will have to deal and to whom every nation will have to give account.

This is also the message of the New Testament. When Paul spoke at Athens on Mars Hill, he told them that God allots every nation its time and space. He draws the map. For example, I believe it was God who brought the British Empire to an end. When I was a boy the school atlas was largely red. It was possible to travel right round the world and never leave British soil. What happened to this great empire? The answer is that Britain washed its hands of God's people, Israel. So God said, 'If Britain can't look after Israel she can't look after anybody,' and within five years the empire went. I believe that was one of the clearest examples of the hand of God.

So it is clear through reading the prophets that God judges other nations by their attitude to his people. I believe the same principle applies today to the Church. God judges people by how they treat the Church. What we do to God's people we do to God. Jesus picked up the same principle, saying that at the final judgement God will say to the nations: 'Whatever you did for one of the least of these brothers of mine, you did for me' (Matthew 25:40). By 'brothers' he means 'my people'. In the same way, when Saul of Tarsus met Jesus on the road to Damascus, he learned how the Lord saw his people. He said, 'Saul, why are you persecuting me?' – when in fact Saul had been persecuting Christians. He was horrified to learn that in persecuting them he was persecuting Christ. But as far as Christ was concerned, persecuting Christians meant persecuting him. So the people of God are the apple of God's eye. Just as the iris of your eye is the most sensitive part of your body, so God is especially sensitive when his people are persecuted.

Now that God's people are in every nation of the world, every nation is having to decide their attitude to God's people. On the Day of Judgement that will be a major factor. This principle comes out in prophet after prophet when they speak to other nations, and that is why most of their prophecies are addressed to the nations that lived around Israel and so had taken up an attitude towards Israel.

So although Obadiah may seem a small and obscure book, it is actually dealing with some fundamental issues of judgement that will affect all the nations of the world.

An outline of Obadiah

The book can be divided into two parts. In the first part (verses 1–14) Obadiah says that one nation is going to be judged – namely, Edom. In the second part (verses 15–21) the prophet sees all the nations being judged.

One nation will be judged (1–14)
The nations destroy Edom (1–9)
Edom despises Israel (10–14)

All nations will be judged (15–21)
Yahweh punishes the nations (15–16)
Israel possesses Edom (17–21)

One nation will be judged (1–14)

The nations destroy Edom (1–9)

Edom literally means 'red'. The city is made up of red sandstone, but that is not why it is called 'red' (Edomites were descended from red-headed Esau). Its location is on the eastern side of the rift valley of Arabah. Its two major cities are Petra and Bosrah, both monuments to man's ability to build.

But Obadiah tells the Edomites that the nations are going to destroy them, and that unlike burglars, who just take the things they are interested in, they will take everything, including their territory. He tells them that God hates pride in men. Pride is almost an invitation to God to bring that man low, for to be proud is to have a very high view of yourself and a low view of everyone else. If you put yourself up, you have to put others down, even God himself.

Edom despises Israel (10–14)

So Edom's location at the top of Mount Seir was symbolic of its attitude to the nations that surrounded it, and to Israel in particular. The Edomites were direct descendants of Esau who, of course, had sold his birthright to Jacob and was in conflict with his twin brother for most of his life. Esau's descendants had settled on the east side of the rift valley and Jacob's descendants settled on the west side. In Deuteronomy God forbade Israel to have a wrong attitude to Edom because Esau was Jacob's brother. This is why Obadiah tells Edom that she should not have treated her brother as she did. But Edom's attitude to Israel was aggressive. We read in Numbers and Deuteronomy that they refused to allow Moses and the Israelites safe passage through their land.

This antipathy was also seen when the empire of Israel began to crumble in King David's day. The Edomites rose up and joined in with anybody who attacked Jerusalem or Israel – whether Philistines, Arabs, or later, the Babylonians. The Babylonians were a very barbaric people. But the Edomites joined in and egged them on. When the Arabs attacked Jerusalem, the Edomites joined them. The hatred and jealousy and resentment of centuries came out. When the Philistines came against Jerusalem, the Edomites joined them. They took every opportunity to support others, perhaps because they weren't strong enough themselves.

On three occasions God says 'You should not' concerning their behaviour (12, 13, 14) and tells them that their disobedience will be punished.

An obvious question arises. Did the Edomites hear what Obadiah said? And if they heard it, did they heed it?

The first part of the prophecy is about Edom, but halfway through Obadiah changes from the third person to the second. So it seems that he had the courage to go to Petra to give the message in person. But there is no record of their having heeded the words – in fact, just the opposite. When the Babylonians attacked Jerusalem in 587 BC, they were egged on by the Edomites (Psalm 137:7).

Furthermore, other prophets also spoke against Edom. Isaiah 21, Jeremiah 49 and Ezekiel 25 all condemn Edom, with Isaiah using language similar to that of Obadiah to underline God's determination to judge. So since the message of Obadiah and the other prophets was ignored, God's judgement fell.

History records that in the sixth century BC the Arabs attacked them and they had to flee their cities and move across the rift valley into the Negev Desert to live as Bedouins. By 450 BC there were no Edomites left in their former land, and by 312 BC Petra was in the hands of the Nabateans. The Negev was renamed Idumea after the arrival of the Edomites. The Edomites were forcibly Judaized by Hyrcanus, so that Judaism became their official religion, though they retained their distinctive racial characteristics.

Edomites reappear in the New Testament. Herod the Great (featured in the infancy narrative in Mathhew's Gospel) was from Idumea. He asked Julius Caesar if he would sell him the throne of Israel in 37 BC, and so the king of Israel was an Edomite! His people's heritage of great buildings became the inspiration for the building projects for which he was famous. This is why he built so many palaces, including one on Masada, as impregnable as the great temples of Petra.

So when the Wise Men came asking where they could find the new-born King of the Jews, Herod was angry. He didn't want a Jew on his throne, for Edom had conquered! So this was behind his slaughter of every boy under two years of age in Bethlehem.

It was his son who killed John the Baptist and to whom Jesus had nothing to say at his trial. His grandson was the Herod who was responsible for the death of James and was eaten by worms (see Acts 12). His great-grandson was a man called Agrippa who died in AD 100 without children.

So the Edomites disappeared. There isn't a single Edomite in the world today, thus fulfilling Obadiah's prophecy. God takes his time judging people. It was 910 years from the time of Obadiah to their final disappearance. From this we can learn two clear lessons concerning God's judgement.

IT TAKES TIME

> Though the mills of God grind slowly,
> Yet they grind exceeding small;
> Though with patience he stands waiting,
> With exactness grinds he all.
>
> *Friedrich von Logau (1604–55)*

God takes his time. He is slow to anger, but when he says he will do it, he will do it – maybe a thousand years later, but he will do it. Where is Edom today? Gone. Where is Israel today? Back in her land.

GOD JUDGES THOSE WHO HURT HIS PEOPLE

God had said to Abraham, 'I will bless those who bless you, and whoever curses you I will curse' (Genesis 12:). God has two peoples in the world today: Israel and the Church. To attack either is to hurt him.

All nations will be judged (15–21)

Edom is an example of the type of godless nation that has always been hostile to God's people.

Yahweh punishes the nations (15–16)

The reasoning behind the punishment is clear: 'As you have done, so it will be done to you.' The punishment fits the crime. The Philistines are also mentioned as deserving God's wrath.

Obadiah saw that one day all nations would be judged. The God of Israel will hold every nation responsible, especially for their attitude to his people.

Israel possesses Edom (17–21)

One day, Israel will possess Edom. Edom is specifically included as a part of the land that God promised to his people – so one day they must have it, and Obadiah saw that. He saw that there would be no survivors from the house of Edom, and that their land would be possessed by its true owners. He saw Israel expanding to the north into Ephraim and Samaria, to the south into the Negev, to the east into the Edom hills and as far as the Mediterranean coast in the west.

What has all this got to do with us?

First, we must note that there is a Jacob and an Esau in every one of us. In the Epistle to the Hebrews Christians are told not to be like Esau, who sold his birthright for a pot of soup, and wept afterwards. He was full of regret and remorse, but he was never able to repent.

Instead we must be a Jacob. He wrestled with God until God made him lame. But he got the blessing, and it is from Jacob that God's people Israel came. Esau lived for the present, for the immediate satisfaction of his physical desires, and he lost his future. The Esaus of this world live for this world only. They don't care about the future; they are only concerned about the satisfaction of their desires in the present. The Book of Obadiah encourages us to be a Jacob – the man who was broken by God and became a prince, and whose name Israel is now on the map again, after 2,000 years.

Secondly, we learn from this book that when God speaks, he keeps his word. When he says he will do something, he may not do it by next Tuesday, and we may have to wait a thousand years, but if God says he will do it, he will do it, and this is why we can trust his word. So little Obadiah may be called a minor prophet, and certainly he wrote a small book, but everything he said will come true.

Also available in the same series:

Old Testament Book I

The Maker's Instructions

GENESIS, EXODUS, LEVITICUS, NUMBERS AND
DEUTERONOMY

The Maker's Instructions tells of the formation of the world, the
beginnings of God's chosen people and of how they were to
live for him. Still highly relevant today, these books of the
Bible are crucial to understanding God's plan for those who are
to walk in his ways. With David Pawson's fresh approach to
the Bible, both familiar stories and little-known sections are
brought to life.

Old Testament Book II

A Land and a Kingdom

JOSHUA, JUDGES, RUTH, 1 AND 2 SAMUEL,
1 AND 2 KINGS

A Land and a Kingdom tells of the conquest of Canaan by the
Israelites, settled life under the 'judges' and the glorious and
turbulent years of the kings of Israel and Judah. David Pawson
searches out their meaning for those who seek to follow the
Lord today.

Old Testament Book III

Poems of Worship and Wisdom

PSALMS, SONG OF SOLOMON, PROVERBS,
ECCLESIASTES, JOB

Poems of Worship and Wisdom focuses on the poetic books in the Bible. David Pawson explores the treasure trove of the Psalms and searches out God's message for his people in the wisdom books.

New Testament Book I

The Hinge of History

MATTHEW, MARK, LUKE, JOHN AND ACTS

The Hinge of History unfolds the 'Jesus story' which has fascinated so many people over the last two thousand years, and is so central to the Christian faith. David Pawson's extensive research, valuable insights and accessible style will open up the Bible to a new generation.

New Testament Book II

The Thirteenth Apostle

THESSALONIANS, CORINTHIANS, GALATIANS, ROMANS,
EPHESIANS, COLOSSIANS, PHILEMON, PHILIPPIANS,
TIMOTHY AND TITUS

The Thirteenth Apostle explores the apostle Paul's life, his background and his mission to the Gentiles. David Pawson takes the reader on an exciting discovery tour of this great New Testament writer.

Forthcoming titles:

Old Testament Book V: The Struggle to Survive
New Testament Book III: Through Suffering to Glory